Praise for *Crossing Life's Bridges* and the Work of Myra Heckenlaible-Gotto

Crossing Life's Bridges is a thorough and thought-provoking look at challenges and a person's approach to navigating them. Myra shares experiences and insights of her journey of self-discovery, as well as her depth of skills when working with her clients. Willing to be both a vulnerable author and an educator, Myra strikes an easy blend that will be helpful to her readers. As a Certified Practitioner of the Equine Gestalt Coaching Method®, Myra brings her unique style to assist her clients alongside her equine partners. Readers are sure to enjoy crossing each bridge to gather her insights.

~ Melisa Pearce
CEO and Founder of Touched by a Horse, Inc®
and the Equine Gestalt Coaching Method®

Myra's heart for serving people and seeking to liberate others from the things that hold them back is so encouraging. How she integrates practical tools with her personal story and experiences is brilliant. This is a great example of how to take self-awareness and put it into action in a way that lets you bring your best to the world.

~ Jeremie Kubicek
Executive Chairman/Co-Founder of GiANT Worldwide

It is always refreshing to find a resource that is both a joy to read and packed with practical applications. As a scholar and practitioner, Myra's many years of personal and professional experiences give her the authority to teach in the way she does. Her own curiosity and positive perspective are apparent as she uses her love and understanding of horses to provide a deeper understanding of the human being.

~ **Dr. Steve Van Bockern**
Professor Emeritus, Education, Augustana University

Knowing Myra both personally and professionally, this book offers what I've long wished for—her wisdom and insight regarding life and its many seasons of change and transition in book form. Having known Myra for nearly ten years, reading this was like listening to her speak—a true gift for anyone in a season of change.

~ **Alyssa Burmeister**
MSW, former mental health therapist,
small business owner and mother to four

What fellow coaches and colleagues are saying about Myra:

Myra is able to follow her intuition and get to the root of the problem. She has a kind and gentle spirit. She is able to create a safe environment, so you're able to let go and release what is not serving you any longer.
~ **Andrea H.**, *Loveland, CO*

Myra's clear, concise style of coaching gives her clients safety and a big space to grow. Her depth and passion for this work helps propel her clients to clarity.
~ **Bethany P.**, *Cadillac, MI*

As a coach Myra embodies kindness, compassion, caring, and joy. It is comforting to be in her presence, and the light in her eyes is not only uplifting but reassuring, indicative of hope and the knowledge that the client has someone who is present, wise, and has your back.
~ **Sharon M.**, *Alberta, Canada*

A person could never go wrong sitting across from Myra. She's there every step of the way with deep compassion. The outside world drops away the moment you sit across from her.

~ **Angie P.**, *Crossfield, AB*

Myra empowers her clients and combines her work beautifully with the horses in a way that is truly transformative.

~ **Adrianna A.**, *Cave Creek, AZ*

What past clients have to say after attending one of Myra's workshops or retreats (For privacy, only first names listed):

The retreat offered me a chance to slow down, relax, and learn more about myself. I felt the healing power of self-care. Taking care of my own needs benefits my family and friends. The presence of horses was incredibly healing.

~ **Tressa**

This experience really helped me get out of my head and come back to the center of my spirit.

~ **Patricia**

Myra's support and insights gave me so much to think about and helped me process my grief and start healing.

~ **Terri**

Myra helped me get over a hurdle that has long been in the road for me. She and Royal understood my anger, hurt, and frustration of feeling like I had no voice. Royal made me realize I need to ground myself and be determined to make myself heard.

~ **Paula**

The biggest and greatest gift I was given through this experience was discovering I can take care of me.

~ **Kim**

The horses found the joy deep inside my heart and gave me permission to let go of my pain. I find joy now about who I am.

~ Stephanie

My sincere gratitude to you for my experience with you and Ginger at Crossing Life's Bridges. Your coaching excellence has helped me move through a major obstacle in my life. Ginger was a solace I haven't felt in years.

~ Becky

Crossing Life's Bridges

Crossing Life's Bridges

Navigating Transitions and Creating Shifts
... Bit by Bit

Myra Heckenlaible-Gotto, EdD

THRONE
PUBLISHING GROUP

Throne Publishing Group
1601 East 69th St N Suite 306
Sioux Falls, SD 57108
ThronePG.com

Dedication

To my husband, Kevin, and our sons,
Lukas, Levi, and Jacob

Thank you for your unending love and
for believing in and supporting my dreams.

You all willingly share your caring hearts,
great sense of humor, and playfulness with others,
making this world a better place.

I treasure the time we spend together.

Love you lots!

Table of Contents

Acknowledgements

There have been so many extraordinary people who have mentored me or walked alongside me on this incredible adventure called life. For this, I'll be forever grateful to you.

I want to give a special recognition to the following people:

No matter how much formal training I've had, the most authentic, genuine teachers have been the children, adolescents, and adults who had the courage to share their stories and face their challenges, coming out stronger on the other end. To all of you, words cannot begin to express my gratitude for what you've taught me about life and perseverance. I thank God for granting me the opportunity to be a small part of your journey.

Because every Equine Gestalt Coaching session is a personal, intimate process, each person's experience is unique.

I'd like to express my deep appreciation to you—Sheila, Randy, Becky, Rhonda, Patricia, Peggy Lou, Stephanie, September—for sharing your story and offering others a glimpse of the incredible guidance and healing horses can offer humans. Your words will touch and resonate with many people. From the bottom of my heart (and my horses'), thank you.

Thank you to GiANT Worldwide for granting me permission to share a few of your powerful yet simple leadership tools in my book. The world is a better place thanks to people like you who strive to grow and help others grow, personally and professionally. I'd like to offer my special thanks to Hunter Hodge for sharing the gift of time to listen patiently to my many ideas and going the extra mile to support my vision. To all of you at GiANT, you continue to inspire me with your passion for uplifting others. I appreciate you.

Having an idea and turning it into a book is internally challenging and more rewarding than I could have ever imagined. None of this would have been possible without the amazing team at Throne Publishing Group. I want to sincerely thank all of you. Without hesitation, you share your hearts and exceptional talents. I want to give a special thank you to Jeremy Brown, Chris Tracy, and Marguerite Bonnett for encouraging my passion, believing in my purpose, and cheering me on throughout this journey. I look forward to what's ahead.

To my parents, Walter and Annetta Heckenlaible, thank you for your love and support throughout my life. The gift of growing up on the farm not only gave me wonderful adventures and special memories but also provided me with a solid foundation that continues to ground me as I follow the dreams God placed in my heart. I'm deeply grateful to you.

Introduction

In my heart, I still consider myself that curious little farm girl from South Dakota. But there was a time when I got caught up in the busyness of life and lost sight of her. I minimized or rationalized my life experiences, chalking it up to "everybody goes through this." I let my humanness get in the way and tried to manage things on my own.

It took me years to realize the importance of slowing down and taking time to take care of me. I'm beyond grateful to have come full circle, reconnecting with that little farm girl. How did this happen? By embracing child-like faith and trusting in God's timing, not mine.

It would be easy for me to say, "life happens." It's true. Life does happen. But we can choose to be active participants, not just casual bystanders.

We all have bridges to cross—some are emotional or mental, some are relational, whereas others are physical. These transitions in life may be anticipated or totally unexpected, leaving us reeling and uncertain which direction to turn. The little voices of worry, fear, and doubt may whisper in our ears, holding us back from moving forward.

But we're not alone. We can reach out to others for encouragement, guidance, and support.

In this book, you'll hear my heart and passion for continual growth through both educational and experiential methods and approaches. Using our mind to learn and understand and being present to fully experience life is a beautiful dance.

You'll hear my stories and stories from people whose lives were touched and transformed by powerful interactions with horses.

My hope is that you'll continue to stretch and grow throughout your personal and professional life as you achieve the following:

- Deepen your self-awareness
- Let go of things that hold you back
- Identify, embrace, and utilize the priceless God-given gifts within you to serve others
- Create a ripple effect of kindness
- Take the time to take care of you

I invite you to embark on the journey of crossing your life's bridges with faith, hope, and love ... bit by bit.

CHAPTER ONE

A Slow Transition from a Little Farm Girl to a Robot (and back)

Life is short and there will always be dirty dishes ... so let's dance.

~ James Howe

Oh, how I loved growing up on the farm. The memories bring a smile to my face as I take a deep, relaxing breath.

THE CURIOUS LITTLE FARM GIRL

One of my favorite places on the farm was the rock pile. Every spring, we went out into the fields to remove any large rocks that could damage the farm equipment. When we picked rocks, we rode on the hayrack out to the field, picked up and loaded the rocks on the hayrack, then unloaded them on the rock pile. If any other person looked at the rock pile, they'd say it was a lone tree trunk surrounded by rocks in the cattle pasture.

Visually, that was true. But, to me, that rock pile had a much deeper meaning and left a lasting impression on me.

You see, I spent a lot of time on that rock pile. It was a place of peace and calmness where I could just be me. Sometimes I sat on the rock pile and listened to whatever sounds nature made. Other times I wrote poems or stories on little three-inch squares, which I bound together with yarn.

The rock pile became a special place that anchored me, giving me the space to reflect and recharge. I can't even count how many times my rock pile memories have been my "happy place" when I needed to relax, find peace, or quiet myself. Even at a young age, I was so curious as to what lies beneath the surface. On the outside, the rocks appeared dull, worn, and a bit dirty from lying on the ground. But the best part was finding out what treasures lie within the rocks beneath that hard, strong surface that protected whatever was inside. I couldn't wait to find out. I closed my eyes and used all my strength to smash the rocks together.

When I opened my eyes, I was so excited to see the colors inside. Little flecks of silver and gold flickered and sparkled in the sunlight. Each rock had its own unique style and held a hidden treasure, if I was willing to look close enough.

THE COMPASSIONATE LITTLE FARM GIRL

As far back as I can remember, I've always been very aware of and sensitive to the emotional states of others. Whether I was observing others or participating in a group, I could usually figure out the dynamics within the relationships. Growing up, I remember multiple situations where I felt the need to stand up for someone if I felt they were being treated unfairly or poorly. Although I didn't like conflict, I tended to take care of others.

When I was in fifth grade, my eyesight started becoming progressively worse. If the optometrist couldn't find a way to stop my cornea from degenerating, there was a possibility of blindness.

As I watched my parents process the news, I felt responsible for their feelings of sadness and worry. I didn't want to add more stress, so I put on a brave face and rationalized the situation. I remember telling my mom not to worry because I've already seen lots of colors and objects. So, if they described something to me, I'd be able to visualize it in my mind—the simple and concrete thinking of a ten year old.

Given my age, I didn't understand the ramifications of the situation. I just knew I didn't like seeing other people hurting, so I minimized and locked away whatever my mind was processing, and my heart was feeling.

I wanted to make a tough situation positive, so, at age ten, I told my parents I was going to help other children and honor my family name once I earned my doctorate.

THE CONSCIENTIOUS LITTLE FARM GIRL

My parents worked hard for what they had and taught us to take care of our belongings. When I close my eyes, I can still picture our farm. All the outbuildings—the house, the barns, the sheds, the garage—they were well-maintained and painted white with green trim. One or two outbuildings were painted each summer to keep everything looking fresh and clean. The white corral fence took a long time to paint, but it looked amazing when it was done. The lawn was neatly groomed, and everything had its place in the yard. We helped out on the farm with whatever was needed, from gathering eggs to feeding the pigs and cows to hauling and stacking bales to driving the tractors to baking or making meals. Being a good student and participating in school activities were encouraged and supported. Whether I was doing something at home or school, it was always important to me to complete tasks well and thoroughly.

Overall, I'd have to say this little farm girl was carefree, spent most of her time outdoors, and entertained herself in creative ways. Her love of animals, especially horses, was evident. She was confident, compassionate, curious, and outgoing. Working hard in school and at home was important, yet she definitely took time to play and explore. She loved listening to music, dancing, and moving to her own rhythm. She seemed determined to take on the world without letting fear or worry hold her back.

I smile as I remember that little girl.

Remember? It sounds like the little girl was someone from my past. Someone removed from me. Although the experiences were special memories, the dreams, values, and joy inside that little girl were still alive.

I don't remember when it started, but, somewhere along the way, I let her be overshadowed. I ignored her, pushed her down, and basically buried her as the demands and expectations of adulthood came my way. My focus became my family and career. Don't get me wrong, those are important parts of my life. But, somehow, I got caught up in the hustle of life. Without conscious effort, I lost sight of that little girl inside me for many years, and it took a toll.

THE EMERGING ROBOT

Life happened. College. Career. Marriage. Children. Graduate school. Juggling commitments and schedules. Self-care/recharge. Wait a minute. Let's be honest. I know, intellectually, the importance of self-care. However, I didn't believe I needed it or had the extra time to do it. The four years during my doctoral program were a very busy season of life, and my focus was taking care of my family and doing well in graduate school. Given the support and encouragement from my husband and family, I didn't want to let anyone down.

Needless to say, I put a great deal of pressure on myself. When I started my full-time doctoral program, my husband and I had two sons, a two-and-three-quarters year old and a two week old. I was a graduate assistant, my husband commuted forty miles to work, and we built a house, moving into it at the end of the first semester.

To manage everything, a routine was needed. In the morning, my husband commuted to his job while I took the boys to daycare before heading to the university for class, work, or study. At the end of the day, I'd pick up the boys, we'd eat and play as a family, and I'd study after the boys went to bed. The routine seemed to work well, but one very important component was missing—self-care.

To some people, our undertaking seemed crazy. But I was strong-willed and determined, so I pulled up my bootstraps and went full force. Unfortunately, I was unaware how the combination of my personality, life experiences, and choices put into motion the perfect storm, the perfect making of a robot.

Many of you may remember a season when you juggled a career, raised children, and wondered how you ever got through it. But you did. Some of you may be in the thick of it right now. For you, my hope is you give yourself grace and time to take care of you.

AWAKENING DAY

From my perspective, I was juggling my roles and responsibilities as a wife, mother, graduate student, and graduate assistant pretty well. A glimpse of daughter, sister, friend, and colleague was sprinkled in every so often. My planner was organized and color-coded. Without the intentional structure, functioning during this season of life would have been extremely difficult. It gave me the opportunity to survive in the midst of chaos.

In 1994, I was two years into my doctoral program when one of my professors, Dr. Davis, called me into his office. I anticipated he wanted to give me feedback on an assignment or needed assistance on a project.

Nope.

Instead, he asked me to sit down. He calmly yet firmly stated, "You need to get the 'S' off your shirt." As my brain struggled to process what he'd just said, he continued, "You can't continue this pace—supermom, super wife, and super student 24/7—and expect to function."

Needless to say, I was a bit confused. For the first time in a long time, I was speechless. My mind was spinning. My initial feelings were anger and hurt. Tears soon followed. Lots of tears. Tears led to feelings of embarrassment.

I was in denial. I didn't want to accept or admit this was my doing. I wanted to blame someone or something else. But my major professor, Dr. Choi, agreed with him, stating, "We have high expectations because we see something special in you. But you put much higher expectations and pressure on yourself. You need to look in the mirror."

I truly didn't see what I was doing to myself. I was exhausted. I was overwhelmed. I was running on fumes. If I didn't start taking better care of me, I wouldn't be able to be truly present—mentally, emotionally, relationally, physically—in my personal or professional life.

My tendency toward perfectionism while minimizing my own needs was taking a toll.

CALLING UP, NOT OUT © PUB HOUSE, GiANT

To the outside world, I was managing my roles and responsibilities. Our boys were thriving, my husband was doing great, and my graduate work was excelling. I was physically present, programmed to get the job done well. But what others couldn't see was what was going on inside of me. The quicker my mind raced, the less attention I paid to what my body needed and what my emotions and gut were telling me. Unintentionally, I was slowly turning into a robot while ignoring my child-like heart.

It took caring individuals who really saw me as a person, not as one of my multiple roles, willing to address it. With their support and guidance, I became more aware of what was happening to me. If I wanted to be truly present in my personal and professional relationships for years to come, I needed to acknowledge my feelings instead of discounting or minimizing them. I needed to listen to my body and give it time to rest and rejuvenate. I needed to create a healthy rhythm between my personal and professional life.

My graduate professors knew the difference between Calling Up and Calling Out.

One of the GiANT visual tools that describes my experience well is Calling Up, Not Out © Pub House.

Due to my denial and lack of self-awareness at the time, it felt like my professors were calling me out. But, in hindsight, there was no question they were calling me up.

They were "for me." They believed in me. They were willing to support yet challenge me. They wanted me to become the best version of me. The key was that they couldn't do it for me. I needed to do it for myself. But knowing and feeling they were in my corner gave me the courage to face my challenges, let go of unrealistic expectations, and move forward confidently.

If they had called me out, this story would have had a very different ending. I would have felt they were "against me" or possibly "for themselves." They were not trying to dominate me or hinder my growth. In fact, that was the exact opposite of their intention.

This was probably the most challenging yet life-saving lesson I've ever learned. Words cannot express how thankful I am that someone cared enough to have this difficult conversation with me.

Although not everyone is comfortable having these types of conversations, the benefits for individuals, families, and teams are immense. Remember, it takes two to tango. All parties need to be aware of their own communication style and responsible for how they respond. But how they dance together will be based on how well they lead and how well they follow.

TIME TO REPROGRAM

To better understand how this little girl slowly transitioned into a robot, I needed to recognize how my personality and experiences influenced my life and helped me take ownership of my choices.

Although I couldn't change how I was wired or my past experiences, I was able to understand myself better, learn from life's lessons, and make healthy choices in my personal and professional life.

Whether looking at your personal life or professional life, nature, nurture, and choice contribute to the outcome—all of which are depicted by the GiANT visual tool, What Drives Behaviors? © Pub House.

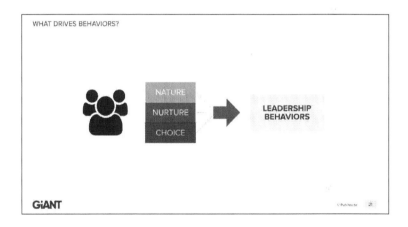

Nature is basically your personality. It is your DNA, your genetic wiring. It's who you are at your core.

Nurture refers to the external influences in your life that affected your growth and development, such as parenting styles, early life experiences, school experiences, faith, and extended family. These interactions have affected your thoughts, feelings, and behaviors.

Choice refers to the act of selecting or making a decision in your life.

Looking back, I realized how nature, nurture, and choice influenced my life.

I can't help but wonder if that little rock pile wasn't the beginning of my life's journey. The journey that revolved around the concepts of curiosity and self-awareness and the gift of grounding myself in stressful situations.

My tendency toward perfectionism reared its head in graduate school, leaving me floundering and feeling like nothing was enough. I pushed myself harder and harder, studying countless hours to make sure I did well and didn't let anyone down.

With all things, when the pendulum swung too far to one end, things got out of sync.

To find some type of rhythm, I needed to take a long look in the mirror. I wanted to find a way to accept, live with, and manage my perfectionistic tendencies, as they weren't going anywhere. It wasn't easy. It took time. It took practice. It took self-compassion and grace.

I'd love to say I don't ever deal with robotic characteristics anymore. But they didn't disappear. However, they can be managed and reprogrammed if I take the time to understand what makes me tick, and I'm intentional in my choices.

Side note: I did find a smoother work-family-play-rest rhythm during the last two years of graduate school. Well, if you don't count having our third son between the end of my course work and the start of my internship, as well as defending my dissertation a semester early as a Christmas gift to myself. I know, just being real. It's a work in progress.

LIFE LESSONS

We all learned lessons from our childhood. Some lessons were hard. Some were easy. Each one of us was created as a unique individual with our own personalities, which, when blended with our experiences, affect our personal and professional relationships as adults. We all have God-given gifts and are given a choice as to how we utilize them.

Taking care of yourself to maintain a healthy life rhythm is a lifelong process. It's imperative to take time to get to know and stay in touch with that person in the mirror. Celebrate the special times and joys and acknowledge the difficult times and pains. Give yourself grace and compassion through the different seasons of your life.

Speaking as a person who survived living as a robot for a few years during my doctoral program, you can't take care of others if you don't take care of yourself. I pray you won't ignore the importance of taking care of yourself because, one day, it may be too late.

It's not selfish to listen to your heart, mind, soul, and body. It's critical you do. Consider the following questions:

- How well do you take care of yourself?
- How often do you take time to truly see, value, and appreciate yourself?

I'm so thankful that Dr. Spenser Davis and Dr. Hee-sook Choi noticed and addressed my tendencies. Their powerful messages, "Get the 'S' off your shirt," and "You need to look in the mirror," continue to have a huge impact on my life and those I serve. I will forever be grateful. Thank you from the bottom of my heart!

BECOME THE ENGINEER OF YOUR TRAIN

I know all too well how the pace and number of commitments we experience during different seasons of our lives leave us overextended and overwhelmed. Figuring out how to respond or function differently adds one more thing to our list. So we do what is familiar. We keep plugging away and rolling down the same track.

A common phrase for people in this situation is, "Stop the train. I want to get off." There were plenty of times in my life when I wanted to jump off the train, whether it was moving or not. But the fear of the unknown and the thought of such a sudden change terrified me and held me captive.

It's possible we may need to get off the train. It's also possible to stay on the train but make an intentional shift and switch tracks. We may need to slow the engine down a bit to catch our breath, regroup, and recharge our battery.

Years ago, I would have said it sounds great in theory, but it's just not possible. My motto was, "Pull up your bootstraps and keep going." There were times when I needed to pull up my bootstraps, just not 24/7.

Here's what I learned along the way.

We'll always have commitments, but once we understand ourselves better, we'll be better equipped to drive the train. I've learned that it's possible (and healthy) to slow the train and even switch tracks. But I didn't learn this overnight. And I'm still learning.

Jumping off the train isn't an easy or simple process. It takes time and effort. Maybe that's why I didn't do it sooner. I didn't believe I could fit one more thing into my schedule. What I understand now is that life would have been a bit easier, and I would have been more present, if I had slowed down. I still have a tendency to jump on fast-moving trains, but it doesn't take me as long to figure out how to slow them down.

Deepening our self-awareness, letting go of things that get in our way and hold us back, and fully embracing our

God-given strengths are some of the most precious gifts we can give ourselves.

————————— **CLIENT STORY** —————————

I had the opportunity to participate in several equine coaching sessions with Myra, being paired with different horses while building on topics we discussed. I felt coming to Crossing Life's Bridges was the direction God nudged me in. He knew what I needed.

My experience was nothing short of amazing. I was able to interact with four different horses. Given their calming presence, these gentle giants shared their huge hearts and spirit. Using their intuition and restorative presence, they were able to see inside my heart, encouraging me on my healing journey. Each one helped teach me something unique about myself.

- *Ginger taught me I needed to trust my heart and my gut.*
- *Gabriel taught me to value, trust, and respect myself. By looking toward the light, I could see new beginnings.*
- *Grooming Royal was a symbolic experience for me. By getting rid of the dirt and shedding things I no longer want or need to carry in my heart, things can become shiny, polished, and smooth. I was so at peace. My heart, head, and gut were aligned.*
- *Annie taught me the importance of grounding myself in my truth. While I was walking and repeating three positive traits, she stepped in front of me, allowing me to stop and truly embrace the three words that are at the core of who I am: loving, caring, and giving.*

So, as you can see, horses have so many gifts. My heart and life have been forever changed because of them.
Thank you, Myra. This experience truly changed my life!

~ Sheila

EVERY DAY IS A GIFT

Why do I share all of this? Because I have seen, experienced, and continue to be amazed by the transformational shifts that can occur when you deepen your self-awareness and let go of things that hold you back.

When your heart, mind, and soul are open, the following benefits are possible:

- Understanding what makes you tick
- Identifying your strengths and challenges
- Improving your communication skills
- Enhancing your leadership skills
- Strengthening your personal and professional relationships
- Achieving a smoother work-home-play-rest rhythm
- Embracing and utilizing your God-given gifts
- Feeling a sense of freedom
- Being your authentic self
- Giving yourself grace and compassion

Throughout our lives, we're given the opportunity to continually stretch and grow—if we're open and willing. Each morning when we open our eyes, we're given a gift, the gift of sharing our time and talents to make someone else's day a little brighter.

When we take time to recharge and reconnect with ourselves, we have the energy to keep making a positive difference in not only our lives but also in the lives of others.

When we acknowledge and appreciate our individual gifts, we become stronger together, setting into motion a ripple effect with each small positive action.

I'm so grateful that little farm girl was strong-willed, curious, and independent—yet waited patiently for me until I found my way back to her. Unbeknownst to me, she was teaching me valuable lessons and giving me a sneak peek into my tendencies this whole time.

During my childhood, I learned some major life lessons:

- I understood the importance of having something to anchor me when times got rocky. I also understood the importance of looking beyond the surface of a relationship, an experience, or a situation. If I truly wanted to see and understand the person in the mirror, I needed to take the time to dig deeper.
- My heart and desire to help others were fueled by my experiences and continued throughout my personal and professional life. However, I needed to learn to take care of my own needs and not minimize my feelings or experiences if I wanted to continue to serve others.
- Given my wiring and experiences, I developed a strong work ethic, took pride in my work, and became well-organized, which gave me a sense of accomplishment. But I couldn't have anticipated the impact these behaviors would have when taken to the extreme. I needed to learn to manage my tendency toward perfectionism to find a healthy rhythm in my life.

Sometimes it's the small and simple things that teach us the most valuable lessons.

QUESTIONS FOR REFLECTION

1. The hidden treasure inside you is worth looking for, finding, and embracing. What might you find if you looked close enough?
2. What differences do you notice personally and professionally when you're Called Up instead of Called Out?
3. What life lessons did you learn from your childhood?

CHAPTER TWO

Crossing Bridges— One Step at a Time

Here's the truth about life: It's a whirling dance
of light and darkness, joy and sorrow.
Change is inevitable.
You can either learn to move with the music
or stand on the dance floor and complain.
The choice is yours.
I say, "Let's dance!"

~ John Mark Green

In this book, I refer to the different life transitions or experiences we face as *bridges*. These bridges link our past to our future. They provide passage from one time or place to another, as well as facilitate connection and transformation.

Our journey is affected by our personality, life experiences, and the past and present relationships, which have collectively influenced our thoughts, feelings, values, and beliefs. Yet, it is our present reality that will determine how we will ultimately proceed.

No matter our age, gender, socioeconomic status, or geographical location, we have something in common. We will all experience transitions in our lives. These transitions may occur at specific developmental stages, at random moments in time, or in different seasons of life. They can be associated with broad categories such as relationships, emotional or mental health, physical health, geographic location, careers, and aging.

As human beings, we all have bridges to cross. Some of them are anticipated, whereas others are unexpected. Some can be intriguing and exciting. Others can leave us confused and temporarily paralyzed. When the passage across is challenging, a wide range of emotions can emerge, including anxiety, fear, doubt, guilt, frustration, sadness, or anger.

So how do we cross these bridges?

One step at a time.

The passage may be foreign, challenging us to go outside our comfort zone. As we walk this unfamiliar path, we may even lose our footing, causing us to stumble or fall. We may feel out of sync, and self-defeating thoughts can start to emerge.

What's important is we regroup, reach out to others, and regain our footing. We'll find our rhythm when we take time to listen to what our head, heart, and gut are telling us. If we want to continue moving forward, we need to be actively involved in the process. Whether we go over, under, around, or through the bridge, the journey is ours to make.

MY DAD

One of the most difficult bridges I've had to cross was the loss of my dad. I have so many memories and stories. Most bring laughter and a smile to my face, and a few still bring tears.

My dad was a hardworking farmer who took amazing care of my mom, my two older sisters, and me. Dad was a kind, sincere human being who would do anything for anybody. He was a faith-based man who led our family with quiet strength.

He loved music and could be heard singing, humming, or whistling anytime and anywhere. His range was amazing, as he could sing first tenor to bass—all by ear. My favorite was listening to him sing first tenor in his barbershop quartet.

My mother encouraged me to sing a duet with my dad at my wedding. She said one day I'd be glad I did. Initially, I thought singing at my own wedding seemed a bit odd.

However, after Dad walked me down the aisle and gave my hand to my husband, he and I turned toward the congregation to sing a duet, "God, A Woman, and A Man." I wasn't the least bit nervous with him by my side. Let me clarify something. I just shared that my dad was an amazing singer. Although I'm not in the same category, mom was right. This is one memory for which I'm extremely grateful.

When Dad was in his fifties, he began experiencing some health issues. Over the years, I received several calls to come home due to medical concerns. The drive home was nerve-wracking, as I lived 150 miles away. Thankfully, Dad pulled through and bounced back on his feet within a short time.

Then the day came. I got another phone call early in the morning. I remember my gut felt something was different this time. It was right. After all the medical procedures were exhausted, Dad needed hospice care. Given his medical needs, we were told we would have a couple of days with him. My world was shattered.

I think Dad and God knew we all needed a little extra time. We were able to spend almost eleven days of quality time with him. Given his medical condition, his expressive language was impaired. However, my heart was filled with joy when he had no problem saying The Lord's Prayer and singing four-part harmony. I celebrated my forty-seventh birthday with my family in hospice, but I got to hear my dad sing Happy Birthday to me one more time. Bittersweet.

HORSES HELPED ME HEAL

From an early age, I tended to be a caretaker. When challenging situations came up, people looked at me. Unintentionally, a pattern of taking charge, keeping my emotions in check, and making sure things got done was created. So, when Dad passed away, I had a difficult time showing my emotions in front of others. I felt I needed to be strong for everybody else. I used all my strength to keep the feelings locked inside. Given my career path, I knew the importance of acknowledging, experiencing, and walking through the pain, but I kept myself busy, hoping it would just go away. However, all those feelings were still trapped inside of me, just waiting to get out.

After the funeral, I was a mess. I didn't know what direction to turn. I felt numb. I didn't know how to express my emotions. I dragged myself through my daily routine and felt I was turning back into a robot. But then, out of nowhere, feelings of anger, fear, and sadness would overwhelm me. My tone of voice was sharp, and my patience was nonexistent. I'm very aware it wasn't easy being around me.

Several months later, a special mentor encouraged me to be still, to sit in silence, and allow the feelings buried deep inside to surface. I was terrified. I didn't know if I could handle the pain.

The only place I felt I could truly sit in silence and survive was in the barn with the horses. I matter-of-factly told my husband, "I'm going out to the barn and getting rid of this grief once and for all!" It doesn't take a rocket scientist to know how irrational that statement actually sounded, but he wasn't going to debate it with me. Instead, he supported and encouraged me.

Spending time in the barn with the horses was just what I needed. As I approached the barn, my thoughts were spinning, and my body felt like a volcano ready to erupt. When I entered the barn, the horses turned their heads and looked at me. Several of the horses nickered, indicating they were aware of my presence. As I took a deep breath and took in their scent, my body began to tremble. When I looked into their eyes, I felt a wave of emotion rush over me.

Before I could contain it, tears began flowing. I couldn't catch my breath. I asked God for strength. I went over to my sweet Rusty and hugged him as I slowly stroked his neck. He gently lowered his head, placing it close to my heart. As I gave way to the emotions, I felt supported and accepted without any judgment. I didn't have to say a word. I just had to show up—authentic, with no agenda. After some time, a sense of peace came over me. It's hard to explain. My faith, my family, and my horses gave me the space I needed to face the pain and begin to heal.

PUTTING IT ALL TOGETHER

I tend to minimize the bridges in my life, trying to convince myself to pull up my bootstraps as "everybody goes through this" or "it's part of life." Downplaying the impact of these transitions doesn't serve me well. It keeps my heart buried deep inside. In fact, minimizing my thoughts, feelings, beliefs, experiences, and strengths holds me back from continued growth and healing.

As this tendency will not magically disappear, it is important to remain mindful and own my strengths and challenges so I can gain the clarity needed to move forward.

Life isn't easy, but we're never alone. We need to remember it's okay to not be okay. It's okay to not have all the answers. It's okay to make mistakes and learn from them. It's okay to ask for help, remembering we're stronger together.

Many of us have encountered or endured the bridges described below. Please know this is not an exhaustive list. I separated them into broad categories for discussion purposes, yet know they are frequently intertwined, as was the case with the loss of my dad. The time leading up to, during, and after the loss was inundated with bridges to cross—emotional, mental, relational, and physical.

The following broad categories are meant to serve as a framework of real-life scenarios for you to reflect on as you continue your journey.

MENTAL AND EMOTIONAL BRIDGES

To cope well in daily life and within relationships, we typically need a healthy balance between our thoughts and emotions. When you read about mental and emotional health, it is fairly common to see the concepts intertwined. Although they are connected and often interchangeable it's important to briefly share some subtle differences.

The term "mental" typically relates to a person's mind, whereas the term "emotional" typically relates to a person's emotions.

When I talk about mental bridges, I'm referring to how well someone is able to cognitively process and understand information and experiences. This includes the ability to think through a situation and use reasoning skills when making a decision.

When I discuss emotional bridges, I'm referring to how well someone can manage and express emotions that surface after learning or experiencing something. This includes the ability to accept and regulate feelings.

I'm not here to debate this issue. I'm speaking as someone who is a teacher at heart who knows the incredible transformations that occur when we get out of our heads and fully engage in our experiences. I believe growth happens best when we use our mind to learn and understand while being in the present moment so we can fully experience life. Therefore, the overall focus in this section will be to share examples of how mental and emotional bridges collectively impact our lives.

The following mental and emotional concepts can create unsettling thoughts and feelings, interfering with our ability to make positive movement forward if we do not address them:

- *Decision-making*—Given our current reality, multiple options are available at the click of a button. Although we appreciate choices, too many can create stress, feelings of being overwhelmed, and uncertainty. We may hesitate to decide because we don't want to make the "wrong" choice. We may also impulsively decide without considering the people or situation around us. Good news: You *can* reach out and ask others for help.
- *Adapting to change*—We may know things need to be different, but we don't know where to start, what to do, or how to do it. Walking into the unknown can be scary and unpredictable. We may try to convince ourselves it would be better to stay where we are because at least it's familiar. Good news: You *can* create a new healthy rhythm in your life.
- *Utilizing self-talk*—Self-talk is a powerful technique. It can be our best friend or our worst enemy. Depending on the message we give ourselves, it can lift us up or bring us down. Good news: You *can* learn how to shift your mindset by reframing your word choice to empower yourself.
- *Regulating emotions*—When the intensity and frequency of an emotion is at an all-time high, it can feel like we're on a rollercoaster speeding down a mountaintop. If we

try to ignore the feeling, hoping it goes away, it tends to get stronger. Initially, it may be intense, but if we acknowledge and face the feeling, it tends to lose power. Good news: Emotions ebb and flow. With awareness and practice, your emotions *can* stabilize.

- *Self-judgment*—We tend to be our toughest critics. We're quick to judge ourselves when we don't live up to society's expectations and rarely give ourselves the benefit of a doubt. Good news: You *can* learn how to give yourself more grace and self-compassion.

- *Self-awareness*—We get so wrapped up in the daily grind that we don't slow down long enough to truly see how we're doing—until it's too late. Good news: The more aware you become of what makes you tick, the better equipped you'll be to handle the tough situations that come your way. You *will* be able to *live* life, not just be alive.

RELATIONAL BRIDGES

Whether you enjoy being with lots of people or prefer a smaller, more intimate group, we were all created as relational beings. If you stop and think about all the past and present relationships in your life, you may be shocked at the sheer number. Depending on your age, you may have experienced relationships across your lifespan. These relationships can influence and impact our personal, social, and professional lives.

Some of those relationships are healthy and supportive, encouraging continued growth. Other relationships are unhealthy and restrictive, holding us back from who we were created to be.

As we all know, relationships are not perfect. They all come with ups and downs. As we walk through different seasons of life, we find our plans, ideas, goals, and needs shift. With these shifts come growing pains. These growing pains can create barriers between people that did not exist in the past, causing additional stress and tension. Ironically, these pains can also ignite a spark for new growth, adventure, or healing.

The following are types of transitions related to relationships in our life. Many of these I've experienced firsthand. As you skim through the list, I encourage you to reflect on the ones that touch your heart.

- Marriage or a new relationship
- Parenting an infant, child, or adolescent
- Social friends
- Separation/divorce
- Arrival of a new baby
- Loss of a pet
- Aging parents
- Empty nesting
- Professional relationships
- Death of a loved one
- Issues with aging
- Moving away from home

PHYSICAL BRIDGES

When we think about physical bridges, we tend to describe the physical attributes within our body, such as the following:

- Overall health and wellness
- Injuries
- Illnesses
- Disabilities

- Physical changes in our body due to aging
- Dietary changes
- Exercise

When we experience concerns in any of these areas, our lives can turn upside down. Our minds start racing, our emotions become scattered, and our relationships experience added tension and stress.

Physical bridges may also relate to careers or geographical location:

- Where we live
- Distance between where we live and where our support system lives
- Career change
- Job loss
- Physical layout of work environment
- Retirement

It's important to remember not to compare yourself to anyone else. Since I'm working on not minimizing things in my life, I'm going to share a physical bridge that can interfere with my everyday life. It may sound frivolous, but it's not to me.

Although I've mellowed a bit over the years, I'm still fairly competitive and enjoy engaging in physical work and activities. My mind tells me I can still do what I've always done; however, my body may have a different version of the story.

If I don't listen to my body, I risk possible injury. I've learned a thing or two over the years. Healing takes a bit longer these days. Just being real. Owning my need to accommodate or adjust the intensity of my physical activities affects not only my physical health but also my emotional and mental health.

Being aware of the connection between bridges enables us to better take care of all our needs.

Whatever your journey, you can cross whatever bridge comes your way—one step at a time.

QUESTIONS FOR REFLECTION

1. In your life, what type of bridges have you had to cross?
2. Which bridge is currently creating the biggest challenge for you?
3. How can you support yourself or reach out for support as you cross that bridge?

CHAPTER THREE

Trolls Make Lousy Dance Partners

When life tries to bring you down—
Just Dance!

~ Shanna H. Leiker

As human beings, we all have something in common. Life presents us with different paths. Taking into consideration our current life situation and past life experiences, we embark on the next steps in our journey. The path we choose may be smooth, straight, and relatively uneventful, or it may be rugged, full of twists and turns, and earthshaking. Either way, a wide range of emotions and thoughts can creep into our hearts and minds.

Along these paths, there may be bridges. Like most of you, I've had to cross these bridges. Sometimes I walk confidently over, under, around, or through them, whereas, at other times, I hesitate to even take the first step.

So, what holds me back from approaching them or making my way to the other side? Usually, it is related to the feelings I'm experiencing and the thoughts racing through my mind.

Feelings are "normal" and play an important part of our lives. Thoughts can build us up or bring us down. When combined together, our thoughts and feelings can give us the energy, motivation, and confidence to reach new heights, or they can drain our energy, steal our confidence, and hold us captive.

When the intensity and frequency reach a point of interfering with my daily functioning or my ability to move forward, I know it's time to take a deep breath, step back, and acknowledge my feelings and thoughts. I know from experience this can be a daunting task. But owning my current reality gives me the opportunity to let go of things that hold me back from discovering a new rhythm.

IMPACT OF SELF-TALK

I believe there is great value in having a conversation with oneself. For me, these conversations are a combination of our conscious and unconscious thoughts, feelings, and beliefs. Let me briefly share a bit about this topic.

Self-talk is a developmental function that occurs naturally when children are between the ages of two and seven. The purpose of this private speech is for self-guidance and self-regulation of thinking and behavior. It's typically not intended for or directed at anyone else but can frequently be heard when children play or work on a task. In later elementary years, you may not hear this speech as often because the self-talk becomes more internal.

Most of us utilize some form of self-talk into adulthood. When we use self-talk as a strategy, we can quietly process the conversation in our minds, we can whisper or softly mumble the words under our breath, or we can speak the words out loud, depending on our personality and processing style.

Talking to yourself is normal, even if you do it frequently like me. Many times, this internal dialogue occurs naturally in our minds without anybody even noticing it. But there are times I prefer to process my thoughts and feelings out loud. Voicing my thoughts aloud and hearing them seems to offer another perspective. Let me share a word of advice. If you choose to process out loud, you may want to be aware of your surroundings. When I'm deep in thought, I tend to forget there may be others in the area and get some interesting looks!

We know there is a relationship between our use of private speech and our level of success, task performance, and achievement. This is one of the reasons why being aware of the messages you give yourself or you receive from others is critical to daily functioning.

When self-talk is utilized in a healthy manner, it's a powerful tool for processing information, weighing options, building ourselves up, or challenging ourselves to stretch and grow. When we use positive self-talk, we're more likely to build our confidence, increase our self-esteem, achieve our goals, and feel more in control of our feelings and situations in life.

But what happens when the messages we give ourselves aren't positive? No surprise. The outcome is just the opposite. Our thoughts feel chaotic. It's difficult to make decisions. Our self-confidence and self-esteem decrease. We stay stagnant because we don't believe we're capable of anything more. I call these messages that hinder our growth, hold us back, or get in our way, "trolls."

WHAT ARE TROLLS?

For the sake of this book, I'm going to define trolls as these little voices or messages that pop into our minds and interfere with personal growth. Whether these voices are quiet, loud, or anywhere in between, the intent of the words, phrases, or sentences is to hold us back from stretching, growing, or experiencing life to the fullest. This endless looping of messages becomes so familiar that we almost expect to hear them from ourselves or others and start to believe them. Hearing the broken record over and over drains us, leaving us with little energy to challenge it.

Over the years, I've dealt with trolls in both my personal and professional life. Trolls come and go. They tend to show up at different points in my life and in different seasons. But I notice they tend to rear their heads more frequently when I feel vulnerable, embark on a new adventure, or step out of my comfort zone.

It is in these moments that trolls can step on my toes or stomp on my feet. If I don't want this to continue, I need to deepen my self-awareness to find a way to get to know them, understand what drives them, and get a feel for their rhythm so I can choose how to move. I also have the option to leave the dance floor, get a new dance partner, or change the music.

I want to describe some of the more common trolls many of us have met and with whom we may still be conversing. Although our interactions and conversations with these trolls will differ, most of us have met the big ones. These trolls may not completely go away; yet I believe the more we know ourselves and what makes us tick, the better equipped we'll be at leading the dance.

I'm aware it's not fun or easy to acknowledge these trolls. But it's important to know what they are and how they can impact us—because they're lousy dance partners. Good news: *You* can shift your self-messages with awareness, time, and practice.

INTRAPERSONAL TROLLS

To get us all on the same page, let me share my basic definition of intrapersonal trolls. Intrapersonal means "within a person," something that takes place within oneself or one's mind. Trolls are these little voices that whisper to us, typically creating fear, doubt, and worry.

Although it isn't easy to own, I have to admit I've been afraid to step out of my comfort zone, doubted my ability and played small, and worried what others thought of me. None of these things serve me well.

I anticipate most of you understand the impact fear, doubt, and worry can have on your lives.

Trolls come in all shapes and sizes, in predictable and unexpected situations, as ones we know and ones we've never met. It's safe to say trolls like to hang in groups, so you may experience multiple trolls at the same time. As we discussed, all emotions and thoughts serve a purpose; however, when they intensify, occur frequently, and interrupt our daily lives, it would be beneficial to address them—not ignore them. See if you recognize any of them.

THE FEAR TROLL

Let's take a peek at one of the biggest trolls that gets in our way of crossing life's bridges: *fear.* Although each of us has a different threshold level, what we typically find is that, when the intensity, frequency, and duration of fear reach an unhealthy level, fear can stop us in our tracks, leaving us stuck or unable to move. It can feel like we're dragging heavy chains through thick mud as we sink deeper and deeper. The links on the chain are made up of different fears, which can include fear of the unknown, fear of failure, fear of rejection, and fear of being judged.

Just saying these words can create a twinge in my gut and an ache in my heart. As I let out a big sigh, my shoulders slowly roll forward. The fear troll tends to show up more often when I want to stretch and grow, when I don't live in the present moment, and when tasks are overwhelming. The power of fear can quickly debilitate our emotional, mental, and physical health if we aren't paying attention.

Over the years, my clients and I would smile and nod while discussing how awesome it would be if only we had a magic wand. All we'd have to do is say abracadabra, click our heels, and poof, everything would be fine. But it doesn't work that way. Many times, we try to push the feelings of fear down, hoping they'll just disappear. But, somehow, these trolls tend to gain momentum when we don't address them. At times, fear can even cause physical symptoms such as chest pain, nausea, rapid heartbeat, sweating, trembling, or shortness of breath. These symptoms tend to snowball, creating additional concerns.

THE DOUBT TROLL

Meet the doubt troll. This troll often shows up when we're feeling vulnerable. When we're discouraged or lack confidence, it's easy for doubts to emerge in our minds. We begin to wonder if we're good enough, smart enough, strong enough, or brave enough. We question our ability to meet expectations of what we think is possible or what others expect of us.

The doubt troll becomes energized when we begin comparing ourselves to others. Red flashing lights signal to us that we don't measure up. This comparison game takes a toll on us, creating feelings of inadequacy and limiting beliefs. Our conversations with ourselves tend to contain negative statements that deplete our soul and heart. Instead of embracing our strengths, we minimize our strengths and downplay our God-given gifts.

THE WORRY TROLL

When I'm in a familiar environment and tasks are relatively easy, my stress and anxiety are low. When I'm out of my comfort zone, the worry troll tends to come knocking at the door. This troll is closely intertwined with the fear of uncertainty, making us feel restless and unsettled. Our stress level and anxiety start to surge. At times, it erupts like a volcano. At other times, it takes the wind out of our sails, leaving us at the mercy of the wind and waves. We may know it's time to take that step, but it feels like our feet are stuck in cement.

The following topics can create worry for many people: financial security, the past, gossip, relationships, work, aging, bills, health, safety, or past mistakes, to name a few. Most humans can relate to many of these yet respond in different ways. Some people shut down, some act out, and some deny any concerns. We want answers. We ask a ton of what-if questions, which can create excessive worry. Depending on our choice of words, the message may be skewed in a negative direction. Examples would be, "What if I can't live up to their expectations?" or "What if I don't get the job?" However, if the words in these questions are skewed in a positive direction, it can leave people feeling more empowered and hopeful. For example, "What if I exceed expectations?" or "What if a better job comes along?"

INTERPERSONAL TROLLS

Interpersonal refers to something that occurs "between people." Unlike intrapersonal trolls, where we battle the trolls within ourselves, interpersonal trolls are related to past or present relationships. Although our nature—our

DNA—plays an important role in how we are wired, I want to look at the role of nurture.

From an early age, most of our childhood interactions and experiences come from our home, daycare, school, or church environments. We're influenced by people in our home setting, such as parents, siblings, grandparents, extended family, daycare providers, and other significant adults. Our personal growth can also be affected by those who educated and interacted with us within a school or church environment, including teachers, pastors, coaches, and peers.

Some of the interactions and experiences can encourage our curiosity to explore and grow while others interfere with or hinder our growth. Although some say these statements motivated them and provided hope, many remember the words, tone, and inflection of a comment that caused pain and left a scar. It's possible the impact of these statements may not be fully known until we reach adulthood. I cannot tell you how many times I've heard someone share a specific statement they played over and over in their minds for years. These messages tend to stay with us, although they may be out of our awareness.

BE YOU

I grew up in a small farming community with a population of 650 people. Given the size of our community, our high school had one teacher for each subject area. Therefore, teachers were familiar with the families and typically knew who was related to whom. Besides my grandparents, we were the only family in town with the last name of Heckenlaible, so making the connection between my two older sisters and me wasn't too difficult.

On the first day of my ninth-grade English class, I clearly remember a statement my English teacher said to me. While she was taking role, she mentioned that she'd taught my two older siblings. Then she said, "You must be their little sister." I was somewhat annoyed and said, "No, my name is Myra." Obviously, I was their little sister. I wasn't trying to be disrespectful, as I knew she was just making a connection. But, for some reason, it was important to me to have my own identity, not be known as the little sister.

I've always been a pretty independent person and never enjoyed being compared to anyone. It may have been my personality, being the third girl in the family, or a combination of both.

As the years went by, the desire to be my own person and be different became more pronounced. I enjoyed doing things outside the box, engaging in activities that challenged me, and seeing things from a different perspective. Since I embraced my individuality, I didn't mind hearing phrases like "You're unique," "You think differently than most people," or "You're different than other kids." The messages I gave myself after hearing these comments were positive and empowering.

Although I'm not sure when it happened, the whole concept of being different began to shift. As time went on, I realized it wasn't always easy to be the "different" one. Being in this position sometimes created feelings of isolation and loneliness. When the trolls began to chatter, I started to question and doubt myself and wondered if following my heart was the right move. To regain my confidence and embrace my journey, I needed to confront the messages from the trolls.

If the messages given to us (or the ones we give ourselves) are self-defeating, we tend to shrink. Our light stays hidden as we attempt to fit in rather than feel like we belong. There is a big difference between fitting in and belonging. As an adult, I sometimes find myself trying to fit in by changing who I am or not showing up as my true self. But a true sense of belonging is felt when I show up as my authentic self and am accepted for who I am.

How do the messages from the trolls affect the messages we give ourselves? How does our self-talk affect our motivation level, task performance, confidence, and ability to use our gifts?

One of the ways we can do this is by considering the level of support and challenge we give ourselves. Unless we're being intentional and reflect on our own words, we may be unaware of the impact of our own voice. The GiANT visual tool, Support Challenge Matrix © Pub House, can help us identify how self-messages affect us personally and professionally.

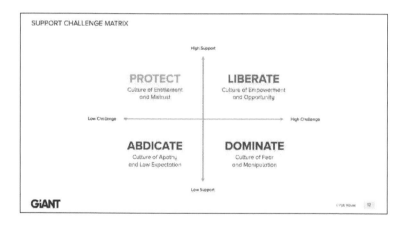

When you look at the Support Challenge Matrix, you'll see it's divided into four quadrants. Each one has its own level of support and challenge, which is linked to a concept and outcome.

To demonstrate the benefit of using this tool on an individual basis, I'm going to be transparent and share how the words and thoughts in my mind affected my performance while writing this book.

As my level of support and challenge fluctuated, I bounced around the matrix. However, the more aware I became of my thoughts and actions, the better I was able to liberate myself.

- **Protect—High Support/Low Challenge.** I've had the desire to write a book for several years. I've had an amazing career working directly with individuals and groups in various settings. Although I felt compelled to share what I've learned, the thought of sharing my words without having the opportunity to engage with people felt foreign and left me feeling a bit vulnerable. Therefore, I found myself not trusting my knowledge and experience. Instead of stepping up and challenging myself to embark on this new journey, I chose to stay within my comfort zone by taking advanced trainings and supporting my love of learning. I was protecting myself. Giving myself high support was positive, yet, when the challenge was low, I wasn't maximizing my God-given gifts to serve others.

- **Abdicate—Low Support/Low Challenge.** This concept didn't come around often, yet found its way to me when I felt overwhelmed and unsure of how to proceed. Instead of digging in, making positive self-affirmations, or giving myself a break, the words used were disempowering and self-critical, leaving me feeling apathetic and ready to walk away. Although it can be healthy to step back and take a break, concerns can emerge if the time away is for an extended period of time.

- **Dominate—Low Support/High Challenge.** There were times when I pushed myself too hard. Instead of taking a break when my head was spinning, or my neck or back was sore, I'd tell myself I couldn't stop until a specified section was done. Although it wasn't fear-based, my perfectionistic tendencies and stubborn streak held me back from letting my thoughts flow freely. When there was high challenge, with a low level of support, the additional pressure and stress dampened my creativity.

- **Liberate—High Support/High Challenge.** I figured out how to give myself grace and compassion when I needed support while holding myself accountable and stepping outside my comfort zone when I needed to be challenged. Being in this quadrant is the best of both worlds. It not only gave me the opportunity to reach new heights but also a soft place to land.

No matter what messages you were given in the past, be aware of the messages you're giving yourself today. When the trolls start to whisper, become sarcastic, or raise their voice, take a deep breath, clear your mind, and tell those little voices they can no longer hold you captive and halt your growth.

Shift the conversation you have with yourself.

Challenge the self-defeating beliefs or feelings; take time to identify, embrace, and utilize your unique gifts; and surround yourself with people who raise you up, not knock you down.

CLIENT STORY

At a critical time of discernment in my life as a pastor, I visited Crossing Life's Bridges and participated in a time of

*guided conversation and reflection with Myra and one of her
horses, Gabriel. As I explored with Myra what was robbing
me of self-confidence and the courage I needed to consider
a big career move, Gabriel responded in the ring next to us
with behavior that, with Myra's guidance, helped me identify unhelpful self-talk and self-doubt. Later in the day, I got
in the ring with Gabriel and Myra, and, on several different
occasions, Gabriel physically but very gently redirected me
when I was trying to create a healthy pathway forward for
myself. My experience with him created the possibility for
personal growth in ways that both humbled me and empowered me. I am forever grateful.*

~ Pastor Randy

QUESTIONS FOR REFLECTION

1) What intrapersonal trolls have whispered to you in the
   past, and how have you quieted them? Which ones continue to chatter in your ear?
2) What interpersonal trolls have held you back? Which
   ones are you ready to let go of?
3) What steps can you take to increase your level of support
   and challenge to liberate yourself?

CHAPTER FOUR

Navigating the Journey

Life isn't about waiting for the storm to pass.
It's about learning how to dance in the rain.

~ Vivian Greene

In the first few chapters, we explored how life transitions and the messages we give ourselves affect our emotions, mental state, relationships, and physical health. Although it was not an exhaustive list, it provided an opportunity for reflection.

Every bridge has its own rhythm, and every troll has its own voice. As humans, we also have a unique rhythm and our own voice; however, in the midst of chaos or transition, we tend to lose our voice and feel out of sync with our day-to-day routine. It's possible to strengthen our voice and get back into a healthy life rhythm by deepening our self-awareness, letting go of things that hold us back, and giving ourselves grace and self-compassion. Although the journey is ours to take, we don't need to walk the path alone.

YOU WON'T CHANGE WHAT YOU TOLERATE

I have a basic philosophy about life—you won't change what you tolerate. This holds true for me personally, as well as professionally. When I'm frustrated, confused, overwhelmed, or stuck (to name just a few), I typically ask myself two questions:

1) Do I like what's going on in my life? Is it working for me? Typically, the answer is no.
2) Am I willing to do something about it? The answer to this question sets the stage for what happens next.

I must admit, I usually hesitate to respond to the second question as I know I'll need to take responsibility for the outcome of my choice. Sometimes it's hard to know how to respond because answering the question means I'll need to dig deep and face some challenging realities. It's like I'm on one of those teeter-totters we had on our school playground, going up and down with every change of thought.

If I say, "Yes, I'm willing to do something about it," I'll need to acknowledge and own things that may be difficult or painful. I'm well aware it takes energy, time, resources, strength, support, and confidence to make a change. It's exactly those reasons that can hold me back—not to mention the word *change*. Change is a funny word to me, as it seems like what I'm doing or thinking is wrong. It's very possible I need to adjust whatever is happening, but change feels like a huge undertaking. To remedy this incongruence in my mind and body, I prefer to shift my behavior, tweak my mindset, or crack a window to new possibilities. It may be a play on words, but I need to believe and feel what I say is true before real movement can happen. Typically, it isn't an easy journey, but the benefits far outweigh the investment.

If I say, "No, I'm too scared," "I don't know where to start," "I don't have the energy," or "There's nothing I can do. It's just the way life is for me," I stay in limbo. As real as these thoughts and feelings are to me, these types of responses disempower me, keep me stuck, and provide excuses for me. As difficult as it is to accept, I may be the one holding myself back. If I choose to stay the course and let life happen *to* me, it is unlikely things will magically change. The message to myself is then, "Well, Myra, welcome to your life."

Otherwise, I could reframe my response to the question by stating a more accurate picture of what's going on inside my mind and heart, such as "I want things to be different, but I'm so confused. I don't know what to do or where to start. I'm exhausted. I'm scared I can't do it. Maybe it's okay to admit I may need some help." When I acknowledge the feelings behind my thoughts, things get real. But that's when real movement is possible.

Life throws us curve balls. If we aren't even willing to swing, we'll strike out. But when we step up to the plate, keep our eyes on the ball, and swing the bat, chances are we'll hit the ball. If it was the right pitch, and our swing was right on, we may even hit a home run.

OPEN DOORS OR CRACK WINDOWS

As I've stated previously, I'm a curious person. I'm also someone who doesn't just jump out of an airplane, even with a parachute. I like to feel things out and look at all possibilities. It drives people crazy, but it's how I process. We all have our own personalities and ways of processing life. What's important is that you take the time to know your style and make it work for you while taking others into consideration.

We've all heard that, when one door closes, another one opens. Depending on the situation, this process can bring up feelings of excitement, anxiety, sadness, or fear. I love to learn and grow, so the idea of new possibilities and opportunities is a huge part of my heart. Yet, part of me may grieve the loss that comes with closing a specific door.

Instead of overwhelming myself, I prefer to crack a window instead of flinging open doors. Given my personality, I may crack a window, close it, open it again, and close it before finally opening it all the way. This tendency has pros and cons, like everything else in the world. Although my first reaction may be to crack a window when facing the unknown, it doesn't mean I can't swing open the door if I feel the time is right.

Bottom line. Whatever bridge comes your way, there isn't one way to cross it. We each decide which path is best for us at that moment in time. The more we know ourselves, the better we'll be at trusting ourselves to make the best decision at that time.

RECONNECT WITH YOURSELF

When we give ourselves the time to really understand what makes us tick, we begin to truly see that person in the mirror. Now I'm not talking about how well your hair is styled, if your make-up is applied correctly, if your beard is well-groomed, or how your outfit looks. I'm talking about making direct eye contact with that person looking back at you, and not for just a fleeting glance. Sounds easy, right? Not so much.

When I was a practicing licensed psychologist, I frequently walked alongside others who were developing a stronger sense of self. The process included identifying the parts that made them proud, as well as the parts they preferred to keep hidden. As they acknowledged their strengths and their challenges, we worked on giving ourselves grace and compassion. This was a journey all its own.

One of the areas we attempted to strengthen was giving ourselves positive affirmations. Most people acknowledge it is easier to list the things we don't do well or don't like. What I found is most people feel uncomfortable giving themselves compliments because they worry others will perceive them as bragging or arrogant. Because it's important to embrace our gifts and love ourselves, we may need guidance, encouragement, and support to practice this skill.

When clients became more comfortable and confident in sharing their positive self-affirmations, I offered them a mirror. The mirror provided a more personal opportunity to practice in a supportive environment in the presence of someone who believed in them. As the clients took the mirror, I noticed their bodies shifted in the chair as their eyes looked everywhere except in the mirror. Their voice levels dropped while their pitch, tone, and cadence fluctuated drastically. To help them relax and stay present, I reminded them to use their senses to ground themselves.

If needed, I offered to demo the exercise. One specific example stands out in my mind. As I took the mirror, I walked through the steps of taking deep breaths to ground myself. When I brought the mirror up to my face, I noticed my eyes began to shift, I felt a bit self-conscious, and a sense of uncertainty emerged. I hesitated. After a few seconds, I was able to give myself positive affirmations using a soft voice. I was a bit surprised at my reaction, as I'd done this exercise multiple times. A little grin crept across my face while a nervous laugh could be heard. As I lowered the mirror, I looked at my client with a deeper sense of empathy. We shared a grin. This exercise was a great reminder that being kind to ourselves cannot be taken for granted. It's not automatic. It takes sincerity, practice, and consistency. What a valuable lesson for both of us.

Taking the time to appreciate and value the person in the mirror and taking care of our mental and emotional health are vital parts of life. Doing these things take courage, compassion, consistency, and grace.

Give yourself a gift. Look at the person in the mirror and say, "My eyes are open. I see you." Smile and talk to them like they're your best friend. I'm pretty confident you'll notice a shift.

RELATIONSHIPS ARE LIKE A DANCE

When we begin a personal or professional relationship, it's important to give ourselves time to get to know that person and let them get to know us. Relationships ebb and flow as we develop trust, give and take, push and pull, and show our vulnerabilities. Given individual differences, each person brings unique traits and experiences to the relationship. The interaction is also affected by our ability to manage the whispers of the trolls. I frequently refer to relationships as a dance. Like a dance, a relationship has its own rhythm, tempo, style, and sound.

Several years ago, I taught an undergraduate developmental psychology class. One of the concepts discussed was emotional synchrony, which occurs between a mother and child at birth. Broadly defined, it is the emotional capacity for two people to respond to each other and is an essential part of the bonding process between humans. I believe this concept relates to our relationships at home, at work, and in the community.

Growing up in the Midwest, I was exposed to a variety of music and learned how to dance the country two-step, swing dance, waltz, and polka. All these dances required two people to be in sync with each other. If the movement between them was going to be smooth, the dance partners soon realized they needed to know how to lead and how to follow. If the communication between partners wasn't in sync, it seemed like someone had two left feet, which meant sore toes.

To further explain how this concept applies to everyday life, I like to share the idea of relationships as a dance by giving a little demo in class. Realizing many young adults didn't grow up listening or dancing to the same music I did, I created the following analogy and added some background music to boot.

As you most likely were not in my class, I invite you to pick up your phone and listen to the music discussed below to get a sense of what it may feel like when relationships are out of sync. Visualize and try to experience the following scenarios.

Pretend you're listening to a polka right now. If your personality had the tempo, rhythm, and style of a polka, but the person on the other side of you had the personality of the chicken dance, how easy would it be to move together?

Have you ever been in a relationship where you felt you were doing a polka, and they were doing the chicken dance?

If the interaction between the two of you during this dance represented your relationship,

- Would your communication be clear and collaborative, or would it be passive or aggressive?
- How would others perceive the relationship? Cordial and connected or defensive and rocky?
- Would you feel heard, understood, and valued, or would you feel ignored, misunderstood, and taken for granted?

Now picture one of you dancing a waltz while the other is trying to swing dance. Or maybe one person is doing a country two-step while the other one hears, "Teach me how to Dougie." Some of you may need to look that last one up. My son had to teach me ... or tried!

If the two people involved hope to find a healthy rhythm and work together, they'll need to communicate, collaborate, trust, and respect their individual differences and find a rhythm unique to them.

FIND YOUR RHYTHM

Whether we're dancing solo, with a partner, or in a group, we need to find our own rhythm. The trolls who start to whisper and chatter may be trying to cut in on the dance, making it difficult to navigate the relationship without conflict. But if we choose to ignore or reframe the message, we may decide to switch the music so we can move freely and effortlessly across the floor.

The more dances we learn, the better equipped we'll be at crossing the bridges along our path.

Trust your own rhythm without comparing yourself to others. Relationships, just like dance, take practice. It doesn't mean it'll be easy, but it'll be possible. Trust God's timing—the right song will come at the right time with the right person at the right place. All we need to do is keep dancing.

FIND YOUR VOICE

Although trolls can show up when we least expect them, we can silence their voices when we stand up to them by ignoring, negating, or reframing their message. So how do we quiet the troll's voice so our own voice can be heard? The best way to deal with these trolls is to come face to face with them. That thought can create some anxiety. I hear you. But, if we don't, they'll continue to lead the charge.

Whenever I pictured the troll standing in my way, I envisioned this monster-like creature that was huge, strong, scary, and very unapproachable. Just the anticipated size and strength caused me to shrink back. I didn't have any confidence and wanted to pull out the white flag, waving it frantically to acknowledge my immediate surrender.

What I realized is, when I acknowledged its presence, named it (so it didn't seem so mysterious), and used my inner strength to confront it, the troll didn't have any more power over me. Its power actually decreased. The troll wasn't this big scary monster that needed to be reined in. It was my inner voice, the messages I gave myself, that I needed to learn how to encourage, set healthy boundaries, give grace and understanding, and show compassion.

When I became more assertive by stepping up and leading myself confidently, my voice gained strength and power. Instead of the trolls leading the dance, I decided what music to listen to and what style of dance to do.

Over time the messages and questions I heard began to shift. Instead of questioning with a self-defeating tone, such as "What if it doesn't work?" "What if I'm not good enough?" or "What if someone judges me?," the messages and questions were reframed to an empowering stance, such as "What if it works?" "What if I identified and utilized my strengths and gifts?" "What could happen if I let my light shine?" I invite you to notice the tone underlying the messages you receive and hear. If they're holding you down, I encourage you to reframe them. You'll notice the difference.

—————— CLIENT STORY ——————

The power, majesty, and beauty of a horse are often experienced visually. I've had the honor of experiencing these attributes spiritually. I presented laden with an emotional burden that was weighing so heavily upon me. Realizing I was angry was only part of the situation. I could not decipher what other turmoil I had.

Then she entered my life—auburn hair and a natural grace and beauty that could not escape the eye; she looked at me—almost through me—and she knew me. Her size, although large, was not intimidating but rather almost comforting. Her scent was calming to me. She sized me up well and proceeded to amaze me with her innate abilities. As we walked around the ring, she would carefully step in front of me to stop me. She only did this when I was inwardly delving into my dilemma. Could she possibly be that sensitive to the shift in my energy? I did not analyze; I accepted and processed, and she let me proceed. When I left, I had truly processed my situation.

Could I have done this without Ginger? Obviously not. As a mental health counselor, I can be quite effective at helping others work through their "stuff." When I'm stuck, I get help. Through our time together, Ginger gently but firmly held me to task. Her intuitive sensitivity amazed me. I smiled more than once, as it certainly seemed that Ginger had her own sense of humor also.

Putting human attributes on an equine? You were not there. You did not experience what I did. I strongly encourage you to consider it. I've had two such experiences with Myra and her horses, and each was an amazing healing experience. Trust; I trusted Ginger. A horse can't heal, right? A horse can't pick up on an energy shift, right? A horse can't know what a human needs to heal, right? Best not go there with me. These were spiritual experiences. Yes, it is not only possible, I'm living proof. And I'm so, so grateful.

~ Becky

SUGGESTIONS AS YOU BEGIN YOUR JOURNEY

The following chapters lay out a framework for crossing life's bridges and managing the trolls as you continue to stretch and grow. You can strengthen your relationships at home, work, and play by deepening your self-awareness, letting go of things that hold you back, and actively practicing self-care, giving yourself the opportunity to live your life fully.

Whether you choose to embark on this journey on your own or seek guidance and support, consider the following ideas:

- Emotionally and Mentally
  - Acknowledge and own your feelings instead of stuffing or minimizing them
  - Pay attention to the messages you're giving yourself
  - Embrace an optimistic attitude
  - Share your thoughts and feelings with others
- Relationally
  - Slow down and be more present in your relationships
  - Strengthen your communication with others
  - Create a ripple effect by giving back to others
  - Surround yourself with people who bring you up, not knock you down
- Physically
  - Pay attention to your diet and exercise

- Listen to what your body is telling you
- Appreciate where you are at this time in life
- Live your passion

The beauty in this whole journey: When we identify and truly embrace our God-given gifts and take care of ourselves, we utilize those gifts to serve others, creating a ripple effect of giving.

QUESTIONS FOR REFLECTION

1) What message do you give yourself when you experience a challenging situation? Do your words empower and support you, or do they decrease your confidence and motivation to move forward?
2) How do you shift and regain a healthy rhythm to reconnect with yourself?
3) Think about a relationship in your life you'd like to improve. If you were dancing together with someone, what could you do to be more in sync with each other?

CHAPTER FIVE

Curiosity

May the curiosity in your heart
inspire your dance.

~ Dr. Myra Heckenlaible-Gotto

One of my favorite things about being born and raised in the Midwest was getting the opportunity to experience all four seasons. The transformation of nature was astounding. The arrival of each season sparked my curiosity and creativity. I was pretty good at finding ways to entertain myself. Some of them got me in more trouble than others, but that's a story for another time.

In the spring, there was new growth, fresh beginnings. The grass began to turn green. Little buds sprouted from the limbs and quickly covered the trees with bright green leaves. The birds produced a series of songs and melodies that filled the air. Piglets squealed and scampered as calves kicked up their heels in the pasture.

Although fall has always been my favorite season, one of my fondest childhood memories that fostered my curiosity occurred in the spring. Catching tadpoles! Every spring, frogs would lay eggs in a little pond located in the cattle pasture behind the barn. When the eggs hatched, it seemed like there were a million little tadpoles swimming in the water; squishy little oval bodies with long tails.

After taking off our flip flops, my sisters, cousins, and I slowly made our way across the pond. Our bare feet and toes squished in the mud. Because the water was so murky, it was difficult to see the tadpoles. But if you stood still and watched the ripples in the water, you could track their movement. Frequently, they bumped against our legs as we slowly waded in the water. We cupped our hands and put them beneath the water, slowly swishing them back and forth. When we caught a tadpole, we carefully scooped it up, placed it in our bucket of water, and transported it to a little tank.

Even though I observed their development each year, I was always so fascinated with the transformation process. Each morning, for the next couple of months, I bounced out of bed to peek at the tadpoles to see if anything had changed. Usually, the back legs emerged first, followed by the front legs. Slowly their tails were absorbed into the body. Before you knew it, the tiny frog was ready and equipped to explore land. Watching the progression of the development and growth never got old.

It might seem unusual to compare springtime and tadpoles to curiosity and growth. But, when we reflect on our lives, we can usually see how our natural skills and gifts were connected to and reinforced by the relationships and experiences in our lives. My tadpole adventure from my childhood was one of those examples that reminded me how relationships and experiences nurtured my love of learning and fueled my curiosity.

As the years went by, my curiosity and desire for personal growth deepened. I felt almost driven to continue. But, somewhere along the way, the skills and gifts that flowed naturally during my childhood were not being utilized in my personal life. Instead of being carefree, life became more scheduled. I realize this happens when you enter another season of life, but I lost sight of the little girl. Spending time in nature, being curious and willing to explore, and taking time to rest and play were overshadowed by efforts to juggle the demands and expectations of family and career.

Although neglecting the playfulness and natural curiosity wasn't an intentional act, I needed to take ownership of the impact of my choices. To shift my mindset and do things differently, I needed to slow down and take a long look in the mirror.

That meant asking myself some tough questions:

• Was that little farm girl who loved to hang in nature and catch tadpoles still inside me?
• What adjustments am I committed to making to achieve a better flow among work, family, play, and rest?
• Am I willing to make self-care a priority and not just talk about it?

So was the little farm girl still alive and kicking? She absolutely was. She, along with all her valuable gifts, was waiting patiently to be seen and valued by ME. If I wanted to reconnect with her and discover what other hidden treasures were inside, I had to be willing to create a new path along my journey and make it a priority.

THE JOURNEY BEGINS HERE

Curiosity. The journey begins with being curious. Our level of curiosity naturally increases as questions flood our minds. We may choose to pursue new experiences, discover possibilities, examine relationships, broaden perspectives, or expand learning for continued growth.

My belief is I'm not done stretching and growing until I'm no longer breathing on this earth. Although I may shift my perspectives or create different ways of doing things, it doesn't necessarily mean I'm dissatisfied. I'm just a curious person.

Most people are familiar with the famous quote by Ralph Waldo Emerson, "Life is a journey, not a destination." It's a lifelong process, not a place. The word journey is defined in many ways. The definition that resonates with me is "any course or passage from one stage or experience to another" (yourdictionary.com). It's a movement. This definition does not set strict parameters or expectations but provides space to accommodate a variety of situations or experiences.

To get where we want to go, we'll come across different bridges along the way. Although the topics and situations are endless and unique to everyone, the bridges we discussed in a previous chapter may relate to the following areas: personal growth, healing from a loss, deepening self-awareness, adjusting to new life transitions, letting go of things that hold us back, improving communication skills, or strengthening personal and professional relationships.

Whichever bridge you face, stay curious and keep your heart and mind open to possibilities as you embark on the journey.

Courage. After being in the mental health and educational fields for over thirty-five years, I would agree with this quote from Stephen King, "The scariest moment is always just before you start. After that, things can only get better."

The most challenging step of the journey that can hold us back from even beginning is driven by fear. Whether the journey is anticipated or unexpected, feelings of uncertainty can arise. Humans tend to be creatures of habit. Even if it's something we're looking forward to or working toward, stepping out of our comfort zone isn't always easy. We start to hear the chatter from the trolls trying to draw us into a conversation filled with fear, doubt, or worry. With awareness, strategies, faith, and practice, we can recognize and reframe the negativity of the chatter to find more peace.

When we dig down deep and take hold of our courage, we'll be able to reach out to others for help, guidance, and support. By acknowledging and owning our thoughts and feelings, we'll be on our way to overcoming any roadblocks or obstacles in our way. The most important thing to remember is we're never alone.

Keep asking questions. Curiosity creates confidence. When you ask questions, you may get multiple answers. After sifting through the responses, you'll be able to make the best choice for yourself in that moment. When that issue is resolved, you move on to the next one. Every time you resolve an issue, you build your confidence, one step at a time.

- Ask yourself open-ended questions instead of closed-ended questions. Open-ended questions encourage you to respond from your own point of view. Closed-ended questions limit your responses and ability to share your full thoughts or opinions.
- Every question deserves to be asked.
- It's okay not to have all the answers. If you did, you wouldn't need others. Give yourself a little grace.
- Shift what-if questions from a fear-based to a growth-based mindset.

When things aren't going well, we tend to put a negative spin on what-if questions. This type of questioning can spiral, creating additional stress and worry. Using the following scenarios from my own life, I share a few examples of how I've shifted my perspective on situations by reframing the what-if questions from a fear-based mindset to a *growth-based* mindset. See if you can hear and feel the difference when you read both sets of questions.

My schedule is jam-packed, but I take on more.
- What if I miss an opportunity by saying no?
- What if my colleagues think I'm lazy or not good enough if I say no?
  - *What if I'm more intentional as to what I say yes to?*
  - *What if I block off time for self-care?*

I've experienced a loss in my life, but I don't want people to think I'm not strong enough.
- What if I have to admit I need help?
- What if I lose control of my emotions in front of people?
  - *What if acknowledging my pain could be the beginning of my healing?*
  - *What if I accept the fact that it is okay to not have it all together?*

I know what's in my heart, but I'm afraid I'll make a mistake.
- What if people judge me?
- What if I give everything I have and it's still not enough?
  - *What if I get out of my own way and pursue the dream God placed in my heart?*
  - *What if I could see every opportunity as a stepping-stone?*

Being curious doesn't mean I'm not grateful for what I've been given.
- What if other people think I'm being selfish?
- What if I take on too much and things don't go well?

o *What if my curiosity leads to new opportunities to serve others?*

o *What if my curiosity sparks others to stretch and grow?*

I encourage you to consider your own personal scenarios and determine which type of what-if question you're asking yourself—fear-based or growth-based? The bottom line is that one moves you forward while the other holds you back. The choice is yours.

If your questions lean more toward a fear-based mindset, the following tool may help you clarify what's holding you back.

AM I STANDING IN MY OWN WAY?

When we have the opportunity to step up, we may find ourselves jumping at the chance or shrinking back, hoping nobody notices us. If we're qualified and capable of stepping up, what reason would we have for holding back? Others who know us may be surprised at our reaction. But it's

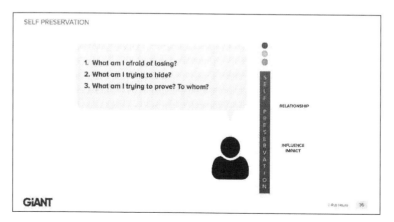

possible they aren't aware of the trolls that whisper in our ears.

On the GiANT visual tool, Self Preservation © Pub House, our eyes quickly notice a large red wall between the person and the words "relationship," "influence," and "impact." This wall of self-preservation creates a barrier between people. If left unresolved, the wall interferes with our ability to communicate and fully connect with others. Given the emotional distance that emerges from this type of interaction, it is difficult to develop trust and understanding within the relationship, hindering any opportunity for influence and impact.

Given the mere height and thickness of this solid wall, its presence can leave us feeling overwhelmed, discouraged, and isolated. It may seem impossible to penetrate. But what if we saw the wall from a different perspective? What if the wall wasn't actually solid?

Is it possible the wall took years to create and was built one brick at a time? Ironically, the same wall that holds us back from true connection with others may provide a sense of safety, a place to let our guard down and protect us when we feel vulnerable. Let's be real. If I asked, "Who enjoys being vulnerable?," I don't believe I'd see fifty people raising their hands yelling, "I do!"

If we want to lower the wall, it's important to understand the individual bricks layered on top of each other. The process takes time, but this visual tool invites us to ask ourselves three questions:

1) What am I afraid of losing?
2) What am I trying to hide?
3) What am I trying to prove? To whom?

These are tough questions, but questions worth asking.

Every time you respond to one of these questions, picture yourself adding a brick to the wall—a wall that may already be two, four, six, or eight feet tall. Although this wall may be a barrier holding us back from showing up in our relationships, it's possible to slowly remove one brick at a time.

The reality is that this wall wasn't created overnight; therefore, it can't be taken down overnight. Good news: *You* can lower the wall, brick by brick, if you actively engage in the process of looking in the mirror, owning your responses, and letting go of the fear, doubt, or worry that holds you back.

Although this isn't an easy process, the growth opportunity is immense.

———— CLIENT STORY ————

I chose to participate in one of Crossing Life's Bridges' workshops after I went through a divorce after twenty-five years of marriage. I felt worthless and had no sense of purpose. During this experience, Myra invited me to enter the round pen with one of her horses. I began to walk around the pen. The horse stood in the middle, just watching me. As I continued to walk, I repeated an empowering statement to myself. Suddenly, I had a feeling of something or someone walking with me. It was her horse. He followed me as I walked to the center of the pen. When I stopped, he stopped. He gently put his head on my shoulder. The feeling of this large gentle animal supporting me and standing with me made me feel I was not alone. This was an amazing feeling. Thank you so much.

~ Rhonda

OPEN HEART AND OPEN MIND

I'm aware how challenging it can be to acknowledge and own our fears and doubts. I'm not talking about sharing them with the world. I'm talking about having an honest conversation with yourself or a trusted confidant. Although this idea may make you uncomfortable, it's important to learn how to become comfortable with being uncomfortable. It's when we give ourselves the grace and space to feel unsettled that things will start to stir inside, igniting the courage and energy to shift.

All we need to do is show up. Easier said than done, at times. No agenda. No roles. No judgment. No comparisons. Just come as you are. Bring your true self—the good, the bad, and the in-between. As humans, we seem to be programmed to be *doing* instead of *being*. Showing up isn't an automatic, natural feat for most people. Each time you show up, the wall of self-preservation will start to come down, brick by brick.

HORSES AND CURIOSITY

Horses are sensitive, feeling-oriented prey animals. Having learned to survive throughout time, horses are highly intuitive and monitor everything in their surroundings. If they sense any incongruence in the environment, their response will be fight, flight, freeze, or return to grazing.

Horses tend to be curious by nature. Although they have different personalities like humans, their innate curiosity can be nurtured by giving them opportunities to discover, experience, and learn new things.

Royal, my thirteen-year-old registered palomino, is very alert and attuned to people and his surroundings. When he is

uncertain about a situation, you'll observe a noticeable shift in his actions, sounds, and body. After he calms down and no longer perceives an imminent threat, he starts to investigate by sniffing and touching with his nose. Each time he's given the opportunity to explore and negate any perceived threat, his confidence increases.

Within the context of my equine coaching sessions, my horses are my active coaching partners. Given their intuitive nature, they quickly sense the different rhythms around them and respond accordingly. They may stand back and observe, approach, withdraw, snort, prance, sniff, ignore, roll, walk alongside, stand strong, or run. Observing the dance between the horse and client in session provides valuable information leading to more in-depth positive coaching questions throughout this experiential process.

You'll never forget the lessons learned from a 1,200-pound horse.

QUESTIONS FOR REFLECTION

1) What is possible if you stay curious?
2) How can you shift your what-if questions from a fear-based to a growth-based mindset?
3) If you reflected on and answered the questions listed on the Self-Preservation visual tool, how might your personal or professional relationships shift?

CHAPTER SIX

Connection

Dance with your heart and your feet will follow.

~ Author Unknown

When describing a word or a phrase, sometimes it's helpful to define what it is not. As you read the following scenario, which commonly occurs, see if you can relate to either the person listening to the conversation or the person sharing the information.

WHAT "BEING PRESENT" IS NOT

Picture yourself in a conversation with someone. Initially, you're fully present; however, after a few minutes, your mind slowly drifts in and out of the conversation, catching just enough of the conversation to nod, smile, and produce a few audible sounds indicating agreement. A million other thoughts run through your mind. The list is endless but may include your "to-do" list, deadlines, financial issues, household chores, scheduling kids' activities, job-related tasks, an upcoming medical or personal appointment, shopping list, or something they said may have triggered a personal memory.

Whether your mind drifts back as quietly as it left, or you suddenly realize you basically spaced out, you're hoping they didn't notice your dazed deer in the headlights look. You automatically start to nod your head and make "uh-huh" or "hmm" sounds again.

Suddenly, there's an awkward silence. As you bring your awareness back to the present situation, you find the person looking at you and awaiting your response. Not having any idea what they asked and too embarrassed to admit it, you pull together random words, hoping they make sense.

Does this sound familiar? Can you recall what it's like being on either side of this conversation? I've been on both ends of this conversation, and it isn't fun on either side.

Unfortunately, this type of interaction is all too common in our everyday lives. It's a classic example of what being present is *not*.

BEING PRESENT

When we're focused and actively engaged in the here and now, we're *being present*. We're fully aware of everything we're experiencing in this moment. Right here. Right now. Our thoughts. Our feelings. Our senses. Our surroundings. It means being free from the internal chatter of the trolls, so we can focus on and be connected to whomever or whatever is directly in front of us.

Whether we're in a conversation with others or spending time alone, being present is an intentional act. Being present is an experience in the here and now. Although some people seem to have a natural gift for being present, it's not automatic. It takes practice. For others, being present may feel like foreign territory. It's a skill that can be strengthened.

To bring you back to a time when you were truly present, I invite you to participate in this little exercise.

Close your eyes. Take a deep breath in through your nose and slowly out through your mouth. Imagine your mind is quiet and relaxed. You're free from all distractions—no phone, no internet, no other people, no agenda. You're not worrying about the past or anticipating the future. Sit with that image for a few minutes. What do you see? What can you hear? What can you touch? What do you smell? What can you taste?

It's likely you envisioned yourself somewhere that brought you peace—a familiar place where you felt safe, relaxed, and carefree. In that moment, you were fully present. Although the actual setting may not be readily available to you, this image, along with the memories evoked, provides a close second.

When life gets too busy, it may be worth taking a few minutes to actively recall this memory. Not only will it bring a smile, but it will also serve as a reminder to slow down and be fully aware of your surroundings, grounding you to the present moment.

Being present anchors us to our present reality and steadies us when the winds pick up.

OUR SENSES ARE A GIFT

When I was growing up on the farm, our swing set sat in our front yard right in front of the lilac bushes. In the spring, when the lilacs were blooming, I would swing high and lean backward, so my head touched the lilacs. I paced my breathing, inhaling through my nose just when my head and the lilac bushes connected. Immediately, the fragrance brought a smile to my face and a sense of peace and joy to my body, heart, and soul.

If you have lilac bushes, you know what I'm talking about. The incredible scent of lilac bushes anchors me. It brings me back to a time when I was carefree in nature without a worry in the world. To recapture that experience, I planted several rows of lilac bushes on our acreage. I may not have a swing set beside the rows of bushes, but being able to visualize the experience, recall the details in my mind, and breathe in the fragrance, I'm reminded to notice what's in front of me.

We don't get time back. Being present gives us the opportunity to take care of our most valuable possession: our time. Being out in nature and noticing what you see, hear, touch, smell, and possibly taste is an amazing experience. It's free. It's accessible to everyone at any time. It's a gift.

MESSAGES FROM WITHIN

In addition to paying attention to what your senses are noticing, consider the following questions:

- How well do you listen to what your body is telling you?
- How well do you listen to your heart?
- How well do you listen to your soul/spirit?
- How well do you listen to your gut?
- How often does your mind get a chance to rest?
- When is the last time you were still and at total peace?
- How well do you truly know that person who is looking back at you in the mirror?
- Are you fully present with and invested in that person in the mirror, or are you just along for the ride?

I know, I ask lots of questions. It's probably because I need to frequently remind myself to pay attention to the person in the mirror. It's important to know who we are at our core.

When we're living in the present moment and aware of everything around us—our thoughts, our feelings, our gut (intuition), our heart, our soul—is it possible we may be uncomfortable? Absolutely. When the present moment is painful or unsettling, we tend to do anything we can to not acknowledge it. We may stuff, ignore, or minimize it. That may seem to work for a while, but usually something happens that strikes a chord, and here we go again. It's exhausting!

Learning to be comfortable with being uncomfortable actually gives us the opportunity to understand, stretch, grow, and let go of things that hold us back or don't serve us anymore. When we take time to truly connect with ourselves, not only will we be able to be the best version of ourselves but we will also be able to shift the relationships in our personal and professional life for the better as well.

BENEFITS OF BEING PRESENT

- Improved Relationships—deeper connections with family and friends, improved communication, stronger collaboration with colleagues, enriched childlike faith
- Improved Health—decreased stress and anxiety, reduced overthinking, greater sense of wellness, and enhanced physical, mental, and emotional health
- Improved Living—more open to experiences, increased playfulness, appreciation for the little things in life, increased curiosity and exploration, living a life with passion and purpose, enhanced creativity

MISSED OPPORTUNITIES WHEN NOT PRESENT

- Relationships—time with family and friends, memories, random acts of kindness
- Life—daily life, healing, efficiency, using God-given gifts to serve others, the beauty of nature, freedom, career opportunities
- Emotional—To feel love, joy, understood; to be seen, valued, heard, appreciated

EMOTIONAL AND PSYCHOLOGICAL SAFETY

Whether we're in a relationship at home, at work, or in the community, we want to feel seen, heard, appreciated, and valued as an individual. We want to feel we belong, not just fit in. We want to feel connected. Whatever relationship we engage in, and whatever environment we enter, we'll be able to bring our best self forward when our emotional well-being is made a priority.

There are two terms you frequently hear that address this issue—emotional safety and psychological safety. These concepts are closely related and are frequently used interchangeably. For the sake of discussion, the following brief descriptions identify the subtle differences between the terms.

Emotional safety is typically understood in the context of a relationship with others, whether it be personal, social, or professional. It is linked to an individual's perception of feeling safe within a relationship.

Psychological safety is typically understood in the context of an environment in which the relationship occurs, such as a workplace.

As both are beneficial and foster a healthy environment, this discussion will focus on the concepts as an integrated whole. The following list is by no means exhaustive, but it contains a few examples of behaviors that promote continued growth. All of us are responsible for creating and cultivating safe spaces. When we show up and are present, amazing things can happen:

- Feeling a sense of acceptance and respect for individual differences
- Ability to speak up with questions, ideas, or concerns without the fear of being criticized or ridiculed
- Feeling free to let our guard down and show our authentic self, including fears, hurts, or desires
- Deepening trust within relationships
- Sharing vulnerabilities without being judged
- Providing compassion and grace
- Taking time to actively listen and engage in conversation
- Recognizing the strengths and gifts each brings to the relationship

THE PERSON IN THE MIRROR

How well do you know that person in the mirror? We spend a lot of time looking at others, but when was the last time you looked in the mirror? Not at your physical appearance, but really looked that person in the eyes. As eyes can convey emotions that may be difficult to express, they have a lot to say if you're willing to listen.

When you look in the mirror, what do you notice? Who do you see? How would you describe that person?

Which do you notice first, the positive traits and characteristics or the negative ones? Speaking from personal experience, as well as professional, I've noticed an interesting pattern. If someone is speaking about their professional life, which somewhat removes them from the person in the mirror, they confidently start with their accomplishments or work skills. But, when speaking about their personal life, most people choose to start with the negative ones and are a bit surprised when they struggle to list positives.

For example, when I ask people to tell me five things they'd like to improve or change about their personal life, they quickly whip off a list. Many times, they want to list more than five. I then switch it around and ask them to share five positive qualities about themselves. Each time I ask this, the person hesitates, takes a deep breath, or makes a comment unrelated to the task at hand. After a short time, they can typically identify two or three but struggle to list five.

What does that say about how we see ourselves? Where we focus our attention?

We need to get a clear picture of our whole self. It's so important to identify our strengths. We all have them. Unless we identify and embrace them, they may be hidden from view and not be utilized to help others.

I grew up believing others may perceive you as bragging or arrogant if you talked about your strengths. What I know now is that there's a big difference between bragging or being arrogant and being humble or proud of yourself.

Below is a skeletal list to help you identify your strengths. If you need a list of words to review, there are resources available online. Without minimizing or overthinking, create a list of your strengths in the following areas:

- What would you consider your personal strengths? (e.g., authentic, courageous, humble, inspirational, optimistic, confident)
- What strengths do you bring to your relationships? (e.g., communicative, patient, trustworthy, caring, compassionate, spontaneous)
- What work-related strengths do you possess? (e.g., dedicated, leader, creative, resourceful, teamwork, detail-oriented)

It is when we acknowledge our strengths—our God-given gifts—that we're better able to serve others and cross bridges.

It's just as important to be honest with ourselves and identify the obstacles in our lives and the things that challenge us and hold us back from moving forward.

Being human, none of us are perfect. We make mistakes. We've done things and said things we wish we could take back. In hindsight, we realize some of our choices may have hurt others and ourselves. We hold back from offering our time or services because we compare ourselves to others and don't think we have something valuable to offer. Ironically, we feel guilty when we don't help.

This cycle will continue if something doesn't interrupt it. It doesn't magically disappear. When we experience thoughts and feelings similar to situations that have created havoc in our lives, those little trolls are energized and start to chatter again.

So what do we do? I like to say we need to find a way to befriend all parts of ourselves: the good, the bad, and the in-between. I don't mean we have to be best friends, but we need to find a way to forgive ourselves for past mistakes and give ourselves grace for not being perfect. It's a process. It's a journey. It's a dance.

By taking responsibility for our choices and learning valuable lessons from our mistakes, we can let go of the past, silence the trolls, live in the here and now, and look forward to the future.

When we get out of our heads and feel into our heart, we'll better understand that person in the mirror.

HORSES AND CONNECTION

Horses have an innate ability to sense how we're showing up in the present moment. Our feelings and emotional state profoundly affect how they respond.

Through the Equine Gestalt Coaching Method®, humans are given the opportunity to engage in an experience where horses use their innate gifts to guide us as we embrace our strengths and face our struggles.

What gifts do horses share?

- Horses offer humans unconditional acceptance while guiding us to our deepest truths.
- Horses live in the present moment. They don't hold onto the past, nor do they worry about the future.
- A horse will never ask you to measure up to expectations, but they will urge you onto the path that serves you.
- Horses do not judge; they accept you where you are.

Horses have a quality similar to a radar detector. They aren't a lie detector, but they can sense incongruence between that which is in your awareness and that which is out of your awareness.

The following story is a beautiful example of how being in the presence of a horse can give us the opportunity to be truly seen.

When children grow up and head off to college, it can be a time of celebration, adjustment, and loss. Although this is a normal developmental milestone, the transition can create a great deal of emotional distress in parents. During an equine gestalt coaching session, the following scenario occurred. Given the experiential process, the client entered the round pen with Ginger, one of my horses. As they walked around the pen, they described their only child's upcoming move. As they talked, I noticed their story contained factual information but stayed clear of any emotions. As Ginger observed this person, her eyes tracked their movement, but she kept her distance.

From my personal experience, I'm aware of the feelings associated with this transition. I encouraged them to share any feelings attached to their child's graduation and upcoming move. Initially, the client said they were excited for and proud of their child. Ginger took a few steps toward the person but turned away. After we processed these feelings, we explored additional feelings that may be underlying the upcoming change. The person's voice, head, and shoulders dropped as they acknowledged feelings of sadness and worry related to the loss of what they knew for eighteen years. Immediately, Ginger's ears perked as she turned her head, locked eyes with the client, and intently walked toward them. The client took a deep breath as tears began to flow.

As Ginger stood quietly at their side, the client was given the space and opportunity to be fully present. At the end of the session, they stated, "It was almost as if Ginger saw me naked. Like she looked right through me and saw my heart."

Being in the presence of a horse gives you the opportunity to come as you are. No judgment. No expectations. Just acceptance. The connection is one of grace, beauty, and peace. To be seen is truly a gift.

——————— CLIENT STORY ———————

I have a job that is people-centered, and when I sent in my registration for equine therapy, I was feeling a little "burned out" from the demands of my job. Also, I was dating someone, and the dating experience was complicated.

When I arrived at Crossing Life Bridges, I met two other people who were participating in the equine therapy program. They had their own journeys, and we shared what brought us to the workshop. We were introduced to the horses, and I was thinking, "Why did I decide to do this?" I was actually intimidated by horses after having a scary childhood experience with one of them. How is it that

I thought this was a good idea? Well, I knew the mental health therapist who was in charge of the equine therapy, and I trusted her. I was also curious about the process. There was one horse that I really responded to, and the same one seemed to have a sense about me.

Since the experience a few years ago, I have thought back many times to what happened for me in the process. And I believe we cannot fool horses. They worked with us to help us with our issues. One time, I was saying something that I thought was true. Actually, I wanted it to be true, but it wasn't. The horse then cut right in front of me as if to say, it's not true. It was a therapeutic moment for me to learn that sometimes I even lie to myself with what I know about my life.

"My" horse was an older horse who had some miles on him. I felt like I was in a similar position in life after doing my job for over twenty years. I was worn, a little jaded, but I had some life wisdom. That horse sensed a lot of things about me. And he taught me about myself. My experience with him helped me to risk being more of myself in the dating relationship. I believe the process of equine therapy really healed me in significant ways. I'm so thankful that I was curious and willing to try it.

Long term, the experience has had profound effects. Not only did I make some lifelong friends with the people who shared the experience, but I learned a lot from the beautiful, intuitive horses. There are times in present day that I quiet down enough to listen to the spirit inside of me. That guides me now. Those horses were able to "know" me in ways I did not even know myself. The experience of having that relationship with a horse has profoundly enriched my life. When I heard the horse who'd been so helpful to me had died, I cried. It felt like I'd lost a loyal, forever friend.

I'll never forget the experience of those three days, and I feel blessed to have had that healing relationship with the horses.

~ *Patricia*

QUESTIONS FOR REFLECTION

1) What is your anchor? What keeps you grounded when life gets too busy?
2) What will you miss if you're not intentional about being present?
3) How would life be different if you found a way to befriend all parts of yourself?

CHAPTER SEVEN

Clarity

We can't always choose the music life plays for us,
but we can choose how we dance to it.

~ Author Unknown

We've explored the benefits of being curious, deepening our self-awareness, and connecting to our present situation. Walking through this process builds a solid foundation for the next step of the journey—gaining clarity in our personal and professional lives.

SNAPSHOT OF YOUR LIFE

Below is a list of questions that can affect everyday life. Depending on your situation and the season of your life, your responses may vary. Whether a specific experience or situation tugs at your heart, confuses your thoughts, or punches you in the gut, or whether it's an opportunity for growth or a time of letting go, you may find yourself in limbo. I invite you to reflect on the following list:

- How do you navigate the relationships in your personal life? (e.g., marriage, significant other, children, friends, adult children, aging parents)

- When an incredible opportunity presents itself, how do you determine if it's a good fit in your current life?
- How can you consistently take care of your emotional, mental, physical, and relational health, given all the demands of daily life?
- How do you move forward after experiencing a loss? (e.g., death, marriage, retirement, identity, job, empty nester)
- When challenges or obstacles arise, how do you stay present to respond instead of react?
- How often do you stay in touch with that person in the mirror?

There are many times when I'm clear and confident in my responses. But, when I find myself at a crossroads, unsure how to respond or what direction to go, I sometimes get a sick feeling in the pit of my stomach. It's like a mixture of frustration, anxiety, uncertainty, sadness, and fear, all rolled into one. My heart aches, literally and figuratively. My muscles become tense. My head starts to throb. My throat begins to tighten. Whether I'm aware of or choose to ignore my physical symptoms, my body is giving me signals that something isn't sitting quite right.

To remove these unwanted symptoms, I try desperately to think of a solution to give myself some peace, some sense of direction. But when I try to think of a solution, my mind either goes blank or runs a thousand miles an hour. Or those trolls start to chatter. I'm an educated person, right? You'd think I should be able to come up with something. Yet the more I try to think of a solution, the more confusing it gets. Does any of this sound familiar?

The example above is a snapshot of what it felt like when I was trying to manage life during graduate school. By nature,

I'm a pretty driven person, so I wanted to excel in both my personal and professional life, as well as make sure everyone else's needs were met. However, it took a few years and a blunt conversation from caring professors for me to realize the impact of my intensity level.

The carefree little farm girl was still there but tucked away down deep inside. People who hadn't known me before graduate school assumed that was the real me because that's the person who showed up. The person who wanted to get things done. The person who didn't want to fail. The person who wanted and knew how to succeed and was rewarded for her efforts. As with any reward system, this pattern of behavior was reinforced.

What they didn't know, and what I didn't show them, was the little farm girl who was carefree and curious. Although she was also highly organized and driven, she was able to maintain a healthy balance. Somewhere along the line, I got caught up in life's demands and expectations. I lost sight of the part of me who experienced life to the fullest—the little girl who embraced life and took in everything her mind, body, and spirit offered.

After learning from life's lessons and deepening my awareness, I'm grateful to have reconnected with her. This time around, I'll take better care of her.

CHALLENGES, OBSTACLES, OR ROADBLOCKS

In every season of life, we're presented with situations that can be seen as challenges, obstacles, or roadblocks. Our perception of a situation is crafted from our genetic make-up and life experiences. We look through our unique lenses to determine how to approach and conquer whatever lies ahead.

To help us gain clarity, we need to identify whether we're facing a challenge, obstacle, or roadblock.

- A challenge is a task that takes a great deal of mental or physical effort to accomplish. I enjoy a challenge if there's an opportunity for learning and growth.
- An obstacle is something that gets in the way or slows down progress. When I approach an obstacle and see the light at the end, I know I'll need to figure out how to go over it, around it, under it, or through it, but it's possible.
- A roadblock is something that blocks or halts our progress. If the roadblock is truly insurmountable, it's important to reevaluate to determine a better path.

Whether a challenge is requiring extra mental or physical effort, or an obstacle is slowing you down, or a roadblock is making you readjust your path, it's important to own them. When you acknowledge them out loud or in writing, they tend to lose power.

When we have open hearts and minds, we unlock our fears, doubts, and worries, opening ourselves up to possibilities. By embracing our strengths and acknowledging what gets in our way, we can move forward. It's at this state of being where clarity begins.

CLARITY BRINGS PEACE

Life stressors affect our level of peace and ability to focus. The GiANT visual tool, Peace Index, © Pub House, can help us clarify which area of our life is interfering with our sense of peace. The Peace Index is a combination of the five concept areas: Purpose (sense of meaning and fulfillment in life), People (relationships in your life), Place (physical location where you live, work, and play), Personal Health (physical, mental, and emotional health), and Provision (you have what you need to live the life you want to live). By giving each concept a score between one and one hundred and dividing by five, you obtain your overall Peace Index score.

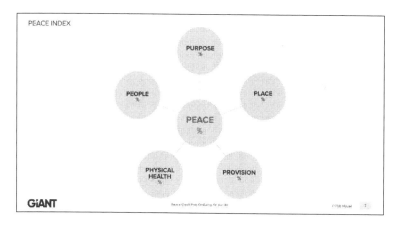

This tool serves as a benchmark to help us narrow in on what is creating discord in our lives at that moment, so we can determine how to move forward. Because life is ever-changing, so will your scores change as you reexamine these areas at different intervals of your journey.

When you view life challenges from a global perspective, it can leave you feeling stuck. In this mindset, it is difficult to see the light at the end of the tunnel when we don't believe any area of our life is healthy and functioning. This way of thinking can lead to feeling hopeless or immobile. By shifting our perspective to specific categories, we can identify our stressors, as well as our strengths. This visual snapshot provides added clarity as we move forward.

SERENITY PRAYER

The Serenity Prayer is a prayer written by the American theologian Reinhold Niebuhr. It is commonly quoted as the following:

> God grant me the serenity to accept the things I cannot change,
> courage to change the things I can, and wisdom to know the difference.

This prayer has spoken to my heart many times and ties into my interpretation of finding clarity. Serenity is a state of calmness, peacefulness, and tranquility. We receive this gift through faith as our head, heart, and soul align.

Accept the things I cannot change

Whether we like it or not, there'll be things in our lives we cannot control, no matter how hard we try. We could spend a ton of time and energy focusing on things we cannot change only to find ourselves even more exhausted, frustrated, or disappointed than when we started.

What do we do?

We focus on the things we *can* change while accepting things we cannot change. Acceptance doesn't mean we like, want, or choose the situation, and we may not agree with it. However, we don't allow circumstances to control us. What we *can* do is adapt and adjust how we respond to the current circumstances. We slow down long enough to take a good look at the challenges and obstacles in our lives. We identify the strengths that can propel us forward. We get a realistic picture of what *is* in our control. We gain clarity.

Courage to change the things I can

Change can be scary. To me, change sounds like a big word, so I prefer instead to shift a little at a time (more on that in the next chapter). Whether we shift or change, it takes courage.

The obstacles may be brand new or something we've experienced for a long time. We may not like them or want them, but they are familiar. Predictable. To step around or over the obstacle may create feelings of uncertainty and fear, so we stay put.

Life is full of changes. There are no manuals or guidelines that tell us exactly how to navigate the obstacles. We can't control external circumstances, but we can be intentional in how we proceed.

The first step is to have the courage to really look at the person in the mirror. You know yourself better than any other human being. With support and guidance, you'll be able to identify your strengths, acknowledge and understand the obstacles in your life, and gain the courage to stand up to and silence the trolls who hold you back.

Wisdom to know the difference

We gain wisdom through experiences. There is no better teacher than experience. As we walk through life, we face situations that challenge us. We learn what works and what doesn't. We increase our understanding of what is healthy for us versus not healthy. We can't control anyone else's choices or actions. When we better understand our potential, we'll be more equipped to overcome the obstacles in our own way. By using our cumulative wisdom, we can make intentional life decisions that empower and propel us forward.

As you continue to be curious and connect with where you are here and now, you'll gain clarity over the situation. Remember:

- Use the information you have at the time to make the best decision you can. The more you know who you are and what you believe in, the easier it'll become.
- Listen to your head, heart, and gut. They all have something to tell you.
- Reach out and ask for help. You don't have to cross life's bridges alone.
- Acknowledge your feelings related to the current situation.
- Be aware of those trolls. Tune them out or reframe their message when they start to chatter.
- Develop a positive mindset.

HORSES AND CLARITY

By nature, horse's eyes are slightly offset to the side of their skull, giving them the ability to see approximately 350 degrees. That is almost four times greater than humans. As you may recall, horses are highly attuned to their environment and utilize their intuition to interact with and relate to the whole world in front of them. This innate gift, in addition to the sheer placement of their eyes, allows them to truly take in the big picture. They don't do tunnel vision.

When we're grappling with the unknown, we tend to replay the same thoughts and messages, hindering our ability to think and process emotions. We just see what's directly in front of us. We stop seeing the big picture. We get tunnel vision. Tunnel vision blinds us to possibilities and limits alternatives. Rather than making progress, we get stuck.

If we're open to the experience, horses are incredible teachers. A teacher who knows how to get our attention and keep it, who can be gentle and supportive, who challenges us to step out of our comfort zone, and who guides us to see things from a different perspective.

You don't have to have horse experience to benefit from what horses have to offer you. All you need to do is show up with an open heart and open mind. Just be you.

If you want to gain clarity, the best teacher for you may be a horse.

—————— *CLIENT STORY* ——————

I was struggling with how I felt about a relationship I was in at the time. Myra invited me to go into the outdoor arena with Rusty, one of her horses. As I started to walk and talk out loud about how I was feeling regarding the relationship, Rusty started to follow me. When I stopped walking, he came next to me and wrapped his head around me. That's when it became clear that it was okay for me to love myself and do what I needed to do for my own happiness. I remember taking a big breath. It was like a weight had been lifted off me.

~ Peggy Lou

QUESTIONS FOR REFLECTION

1. How can gaining clarity help you face challenges, obstacles, or roadblocks and move forward?
2. What is your current Peace Index?
3. When stressors arise, how can you widen your vision to see the bigger picture?

CHAPTER EIGHT

Shift with Intention— Bit by Bit

When you dance, your purpose is not
to get to a certain place on the floor.
It's to enjoy each step along the way.

~ Wayne Dyer

It's no surprise to anyone when I say each one of us was created as a unique individual. Genetically, we were each created with a specific DNA, so we're wired differently from the start. Each one of us was nurtured in a specific environment and experienced different relationships, so we learned ways to respond or react, depending on our circumstances. In addition, we are each given the gift of choice; therefore, we experience the healthy and not so healthy consequences of our choices. Given these things, we move forward in our lives by tweaking, shifting, and changing our rhythm and our dance.

TWEAK, SHIFT, OR CHANGE

Tweak. Shift. Change. Although some people may use these words interchangeably, I believe there is a subtle yet significant difference among them. Maybe I'm intentionally creating a distinction as I always want to have options for movement. For some reason, it's important to me to have choices in my life. I feel less stress and pressure knowing I'm not stuck. No matter what the situation or circumstance, I appreciate having the option to tweak a bit, shift one step at a time, or completely change. This offers a sense of freedom to make the best decisions I can with what's in front of me at the time.

Because each circumstance comes with its own set of variables, there isn't one way that works best for every situation. Given our different experiences and personalities, there really isn't a right way or a wrong way. The beauty is we all get to decide what works best for us given the specific situation at that specific time. If we stay present, neither focusing on the past nor worrying about the future, we will continue to make forward movement, bit by bit.

Let me share how I define these three words as we continue to explore the different bridges in our lives.

Tweak

When I tweak something, I think of needing to make a small adjustment. It's so close to where it needs to be but just needs to be a tad bit different. For example, some of you remember the old transistor radios where you would turn the tuning knob to find the radio station. If there was some crackly static, you could slowly move the knob back and forth to fine-tune the radio to hear the station clearly. Just like that transistor radio, you may only have to tweak something in your life to make it clear and manageable.

Shift

Shifting requires you to make some type of movement, a slight movement in position, direction, thought, belief, or tendency.

These little shifts can make a big difference. The visual that comes to mind is the first car I bought when I graduated from college in 1985. I was thrilled to own a blue five-speed manual Ford Tempo. I know, pretty cool. But I wasn't an expert at driving a stick shift. I needed to pay attention to multiple things simultaneously. I quickly learned the impact of small adjustments as I shifted gears and slowly released the clutch while gently pressing on the accelerator pedal. As each gear had a specific purpose, being aware of which gear I was in, where my next move would be, and when I would shift gears was important. To make a smooth transition from one gear to the next, instead of creating awful grinding noises or being stopped in my tracks, I needed to be intentional in my actions. I needed to find my rhythm.

Learning to master this skill took time and practice, but, after a while, it became automatic.

The same is true for managing transitions and engaging in relationships.

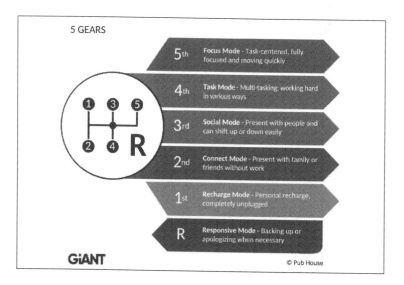

Learning the different levels of connection is vital to healthy relationships. The GiANT tool, 5 Gears © Pub House, is symbolic of these different levels, giving us a better understanding of relationship dynamics. As with a stick shift, there are five gears along with a reverse.

- 1st gear (Recharge)—unplugging and recharging
- 2nd gear (Connect)—connecting with family, friends, or colleagues outside of work
- 3rd gear (Social)—engaging in social interactions with others
- 4th gear (Task)—multitasking and working hard
- 5th gear (Focus)—intently focusing on the task at hand
- R (Reverse)—backing up and starting over or apologizing

Recognizing which gear we're in and understanding the impact it will have on others can help the flow of relationships in any environment. When we master this gear shift, we'll be able to move in and out of relationships smoothly, fine-tuning our steps and rhythm at each gear.

Although rhythm comes naturally to most of us, we'll need to learn how to adjust and adapt to whatever is taking place around us. We need to learn how to shift with intention … bit by bit.

Change

To me, change means creating something different. The change can be larger scale and sudden, or it can come over time with small, gradual alterations. Either way, there is a noticeable difference in where you started, which takes you on a whole new path.

BE INTENTIONAL

When people talk about needing balance in their lives, they typically refer to balancing their work and family commitments. It's important to be aware of how much time and energy we spend in each, but I don't think it's that simple. I think the concepts of play and relaxation need to be part of the equation. Although these two concepts may be able to occur simultaneously with family or possible work–life balance, they need to be recognized as independent factors if we want to be fully alive, not just be alive.

Some people easily incorporate play and relaxation into their daily lives, whereas others give themselves the gift of play and relaxation when or if they have time. Speaking from experience, when or if we have time is code for "it probably won't happen." Why? Because life happens. Unexpected demands pop up every day, consuming our time and energy. Unless we're intentional and make these things a priority, they typically get put on the back burner. So what do we do?

Because these concepts are intertwined, it would be beneficial to put our energy into finding a healthy rhythm between work, family, play, and relaxation. This, in turn, helps us create a lifestyle that can sway to different rhythms and shift with each season of life.

ADJUST YOUR RHYTHM

Things were pretty busy when our boys were young. Our whole family loved sports, so the boys, along with my husband and I, participated in many summer activities. The boys were about three years apart, so their summer activities and schedules were different and sometimes overlapped.

To keep things straight, I created monthly calendars containing all our daily activities and put the calendars on the refrigerator. There was time allotted for work, family, play, and relaxation. It didn't mean we weren't spontaneous. But having a calendar gave us the opportunity to visually see our priorities.

Stepping back, I realize our summer schedule went pretty smoothly because we were intentional about how we used our time. Someone once told me, "I know it's a lot of running, and things get busy. But enjoy it, as the years go by so fast." They were so right.

When we became empty-nesters, we needed to find a new healthy rhythm. I always heard people were bored and had all this free time when the kids were grown and on their own. I thought it would be great not to have a schedule, to be free to do whatever I wanted, whenever I wanted. But that didn't seem to be the case for me. My internal drive to be doing something took over. When I wasn't intentional with my time, I left myself little to no time for just being, which meant little time for play and relaxation.

As I continue my journey, I realize it's important to find a rhythm, no matter the season of life. I'm more aware of how I use my time and continue to adjust when needed. For me, scheduling time for all life's joys—family, play, relaxation, and work—allows me to shift with intention, bit by bit.

BIT BY BIT

People will often ask me what I mean when I say we shift, bit by bit. Bit by bit actually takes on two meanings for me. The first relates to partnering with horses as we explore, discover, and clarify what is in our hearts, minds, and souls. Horses bring to light a whole new awareness in a way that is experiential and nonjudgmental.

The second meaning suggests we do not need to take a big leap to make a difference in our lives. We may think big changes are better than tweaks or shifts, but we often underestimate the power of a tweak or a shift. After taking a small step, we may want to walk that path for some time to get our bearings. When the time is right, we take another step, then another. Each step will be at our own pace. Any forward movement is movement.

When I get a certain feeling in my gut, it's typically a personal growth opportunity or a time of letting go. I tend to think about things for quite some time while at the same time paying a great deal of attention to how it sits within me, how it feels in my heart and soul. Given my faith, I realize, if this stirring continues, it's important to listen and act on it.

But sometimes those old trolls of worry, doubt, or fear of the unknown start knocking at my door and begin to chatter. In fact, they sometimes throw a party I wasn't invited to. I wish I could say I've learned how to completely remove them from my life, but I don't think that's possible. What I believe is the better I know myself, the better I can anticipate, manage, and quiet the chatter, making it easier to move forward with whatever comes my way.

LESSONS LEARNED

It's important to celebrate the progress made and appreciate the lessons learned along the way. The following are a few significant lessons I've learned that continue to help me navigate my way across the bridges. These lessons provide a framework that helps me figure out if I need to tweak, shift, or change something.

Fear and Doubt

As a little farm girl, I don't remember fear or doubt holding me back. I liked to explore the outdoors and believed I could do anything. I was pretty confident and enjoyed taking on a challenge. I loved school and thought learning was fun. School wasn't stressful overall as I was a good student and put time into my studies.

As I entered college, things began to change. I wanted to do well not only for myself but also for my parents. I started listening to and believing the chatter from those little trolls. I remember asking myself, "What if I'm not good enough?" "What if I don't do well and get kicked out of college?" "What would people say?" and "How embarrassing would that be?"

I know it sounds a bit dramatic for someone who was an honor student in high school. But the doubt and fear felt so real. I put so much extra pressure on myself. It was like adding fuel to the fire. After the first semester, I realized college wasn't that much different than high school. My grades reflected my efforts, so I began to relax. Looking back, I understand my fear and doubt played into this new experience, but, by buying into the trolls, the intensity and frequency of my emotions increased. It was important to notice how much time and energy I was giving to unhealthy messages and the emotions attached.

The key words are intensity and frequency. I needed to figure out how to shift my mindset.

Emotions, like waves in the ocean, are always present. When the energy increases, so do the intensity and frequency.

Emotions can surge if left unchecked. People often judge emotions as good or bad based on if they are pleasant or unpleasant. I prefer to see them as clues to what is going on inside and around us. Many times, they're connected to things that matter to us.

So what did I learn?

Whenever I take on something new, it's possible there will be feelings of fear and doubt. Why? Because these feelings are a common and normal part of any new adventure.

In God's Timing

After I had completed my four-year doctoral program in South Dakota, my husband and I moved our sons—ages one, four, and six—to a small rural town in southwest Minnesota, where I practiced as a school psychologist. As my husband's job was in Iowa, he worked from home three days a week and drove to Iowa two days a week. It was quite the schedule, yet we felt we could manage it for three to five years before moving to a larger city, so I could pursue a teaching career at a university. But God had other plans. Instead of moving, we were blessed to raise our sons in this same rural community we have called home for twenty-five years. Who would have thought?

What lesson did I learn?

Continue to follow your dreams, but don't be married to the outcome. Although my plan to teach at the postsecondary level within five years after earning my doctorate didn't happen, I was honored and grateful to have had the opportunity to walk alongside so many incredible children, adolescents, and adults who showed up and had the courage to share their hearts with me. The career shifts over the years enriched my life in more ways than I could have imagined. Yet I held onto my dream in my heart.

After our oldest son's junior year in high school, I had an unexpected opportunity to teach in the school psychology program at the University of South Dakota, where I earned my degree. My dream was coming true, or so I thought. When reality hit me, I knew the timing was wrong. It felt like someone was dangling a carrot in front of me, but I couldn't reach it. If I accepted the position, I'd be 150 miles away from my husband and our boys four days a week. As I didn't feel I could leave the family, and we didn't feel it was fair to uproot the boys, I turned it down.

Being completely transparent, the grief I felt related to the loss of my dream was intense. The sadness, loss of direction, and tears were real. It was really hard. I thought the dream in my heart was long gone. Although I continued to hold onto my dream, the window of opportunity to teach at the college level was growing dim, and, for that, a part of my heart ached.

However, seven years later, when our youngest son was heading to college, I was blessed with an unbelievable opportunity. The timing couldn't have been any better. With my family's support and encouragement, I accepted a one-year visiting assistant professor in psychology position at Augustana University, my alma mater. My dream came true—not in my timing—but God's timing. What a gift. What a humbling experience.

Gentle Reminder

When pursuing the dream God placed in my heart, there were times when I became impatient and tried to figure out ways to accomplish the dream on my own. This only created worry, stress, and disappointment. I needed a gentle reminder or two to wait patiently till the time was right. This wasn't a passive experience just waiting for time to fly. This waiting period was actually an active process of preparing me to walk into my dream, trusting God, and waiting on His timing with a positive attitude and a heart of faith.

Reflecting back, I believe the extra seven years of professional experience enhanced my knowledge and deepened my understanding, making me a stronger teacher. The opportunity to teach undergraduate students at Augie filled the void in my heart. I can't even put into words the joy that experience gave me. For that, I will be forever grateful.

Maybe there's a dream in your heart, but you aren't sure how it'll come to fruition. Given life circumstances, your original dream may need to be tweaked, shifted, or changed. Keep pressing forward, embracing the time, and appreciating all you've been given. You may be surprised by what's right in front of you.

HORSES AND SHIFTING

As prey animals, horses perceive things at a deep level, paying attention to what they sense and feel, not discounting it. Therefore, they respond or react to what's immediately in front of them in the present moment.

Horses can feel everything. Depending on their training, horses are aware of the slightest shift of pressure, which provides signals for upcoming transitions. These subtle movements convey important cues and information. When we're in the saddle, they're very responsive to subtle shifts of our body. If we're constantly shifting around, with absolutely no

intent, the horse may learn to ignore the weight shifts. Thus, the communication is hindered.

Typically, it's the little things that make the biggest difference. We may underestimate how subtle shifts in our thoughts, feelings, behaviors, and attitudes can create new perspectives and understanding.

Horses are honest and real. Their ability to sense where we are at the present moment brings awareness to the congruence or incongruence within us.

Given this new awareness, we can intentionally shift what needs shifting, bit by bit.

CLIENT STORY

The first time I went to a retreat at Crossing Life's Bridges, I didn't know what to expect. But there was a moment where one of her horse's eyes met mine. I could just feel the energy of Ginger's heart connecting with mine. It was as if she said, "I get you. I'm with you. Let your spirit rise above your fear of what is next." To have a horse communicate and empathize with me better than a human being was so healing. After that experience, I felt like I could finally cross the bridges coming my way, holding my head up high.

~ Stephanie

QUESTIONS FOR REFLECTION

1. When you want to make an adjustment in your life, how do you decide if you need to tweak, shift, or change?
2. What dream has been placed in your heart?
3. What life lessons help you navigate your journey across the bridges?

CHAPTER NINE

Find Your Rhythm and Keep Dancing

Sing like no one is listening,
love like you never been hurt,
dance like no one is watching and
live like it is heaven on earth.

~ Mark Twain

Life isn't about doing, it's about *being*. It's about being intentional about how we use our time, how we create meaningful relationships, and how we utilize our gifts that make the journey more important than the destination.

As we navigate our life's journey, we'll experience challenges, come across obstacles, or even face roadblocks. Having a core foundation of knowing who we are and what makes us tick provides a solid platform to step out of our comfort zone and engage in new relationships and experiences. Maintaining a healthy sense of rhythm in our daily lives takes awareness, energy, and commitment.

One of my passions is helping people recharge, unwind, and reignite.

As you may recall from my story, twenty-five years ago, one of my professors gave me an incredible gift when he cared enough to "call me up" during a conversation stating, "You can't take care of others if you don't take care of yourself." Long story short, he was absolutely right. Our conversation continues to stay ever-present on my mind and in my heart. Taking care of ourselves is a habit with no end date.

RECHARGE COMES IN DIFFERENT WAYS

The concept of recharge is necessary for our minds, bodies, and souls to function at their best. Although what we do to recharge may vary, given our different interests and personalities, we all need to fill ourselves back up. Sometimes we must stop and rest before we can continue to move forward.

Whether you prefer a quiet place alone in the mountains, a small gathering with friends, or a large concert event with fifty of your closest friends, these experiences can refuel your body, renew your heart, and realign your head, heart, and soul.

When I'm at home and get to the point of feeling "I'm so done," I know I need to go outside. There are times when my husband says, "You need to go out to the barn." I'm not sure if it's for his sanity or mine—or probably both. But he's right. I'll spend hours with the horses. Even today, breathing in their scent is just intoxicating. I realize you either love the smell of horses or you don't. I happen to love it. I like to tinker in the barn or clean the horse stalls. Sometimes I listen to music, and sometimes I just take in the sounds. People may think I'm a bit crazy, but I find cleaning stalls very therapeutic. It gives me a sense of peace that's hard to explain. What I do know is that being out in nature anchors me.

There are times when I find myself needing to go away from home; sometimes it's a place that's familiar, and sometimes it's a new adventure. Either way, when the time is right, and the place is right, it speaks to my heart, encouraging me to take time for me.

Last fall, I knew I needed to recharge, so I made a reservation for a long weekend getaway at a Bible camp where I was a summer counselor thirty-eight years ago. I felt I needed to reconnect with myself and realign my head, heart, and soul. Being at a place that held a special place in my heart and being in nature-sitting quietly, walking, and deepening my self-awareness-was just what I needed.

There are other times when I feel the need to step out of my comfort zone—to try something different. I search for events that intrigue me and touch my heart. Whether it's to recharge, let go of things that hold me back, or refuel and reignite my passion, the time I give myself to take care of me never disappoints.

No matter the "r" word used, the gift you receive by taking time for you is invaluable. Which of these words resonate with you?

Reignite	Recharge	Realign	Refuel
Renew	Reframe	Rejuvenate	Reclaim
Reconnect	Replenish	Revive	Rekindle
Reawaken	Refresh	Restore	Recreate

IMPORTANCE OF SELF-CARE

The general concept of self-care encourages us to maintain a healthy relationship with ourselves by taking time to do things that help us live well and improve our physical, mental, emotional, and relational health. When we do this, we're better able to dance smoothly in our current personal and professional lives.

We all know and have heard it's beneficial to take care of ourselves. But, when life gets busy, self-care tends to slowly slide down the list. When making it a priority, we remind ourselves and others that our needs are important as well.

By choosing one self-care goal at a time and taking small, incremental steps, we can improve our overall health. The following are some of the benefits of self-care:

- Strengthen relationships with family and friends
- Improve collaborative relationships at work
- Increase efficiency and effectiveness in work performance
- Stabilize emotional health
- Be less susceptible to stress, depression, and anxiety
- Increase mental alertness
- Increase positive thinking
- Improve physical health
- Strengthen immune system
- Lower your risk of illness
- Increase energy
- Improve sleep
- Have confidence in knowing what makes you tick

When we don't take care of ourselves, we're not able to bring our best selves to the table. Our relationships suffer. Our work performance is impacted. We won't have the energy to truly live. By negating the list above, we can identify the consequences of *not* taking care of ourselves.

WE'RE ALL HUMAN

Although none of us are alike, we all have a fundamental concept in common. We're all human. We may not perceive the world the same way, but we all have feelings, needs, thoughts, beliefs, and values that are important to us. We are created to be loving, kind human beings. We all need to be seen, heard, understood, and valued. We all need to love and be loved.

We aren't perfect creatures. We make mistakes. Although it may be difficult to own our mistakes, I never met anyone who didn't make mistakes or who enjoyed making mistakes. None of us do. For those of us who struggle with perfectionistic tendencies, it can be excruciating when we work so hard to get it right, yet it doesn't go as we planned.

Whatever our personality, when things don't go as planned, we make mistakes, or something unexpected happens, our rhythm can be thrown off. We may feel out of sync with ourselves and those around us. This can leave us feeling confused, agitated, or lethargic.

How do we get back into a healthy rhythm? We give ourselves grace, self-compassion, and time to step back and recharge.

RECHARGING LEADS TO RIPPLE EFFECTS

When we take care of ourselves, we'll have the energy and desire to continue to use our God-given gifts to serve others. In return, others may pay it forward, helping someone else and creating a ripple effect.

Our time is a precious gift. It's one thing we can't ever get back. Giving ourselves time to slow down and recharge, we're less likely to go through life just going through the motions. We're less likely to turn into robots—getting the job done but not being fully present. By being more present, we have the ability to respond instead of react.

As long as we're breathing on this earth, we're alive. This alone is a wonderful gift. But what if we truly embraced our uniqueness and shared our gifts with the world? What if we didn't let the past hold us captive? What if we didn't minimize our challenges or gifts?

What if we trusted our gut, acknowledged and owned our strengths as well as our challenges, and found a way to manage the troll's chatter? What if we gave ourselves and others grace and compassion?

Can you imagine what that would be like, being alive AND *living* the life you were given? What a gift. What a blessing. What a life to share with others.

HORSES AND RECHARGE

Horses offer us unconditional acceptance; they do not judge. They guide us to our deepest truths and give us the opportunity to experience what it's like to just be present, not worrying about the past or worrying about the future.

Horses have an innate ability to sense how we're showing up in the present moment. All you need to do is show up, dropping your concerns on the arena floor.

The question is, will you show up? Are you open to seeing things from a different perspective? Will you give yourself the opportunity to experience what your head, heart, and soul are telling you? Will you give yourself the gift of being present, renewing your heart, and recharging your soul?

With their mere presence, horses bring to light our truth and that which is holding us back from living an authentic life. The choice of where we walk with that awareness is then ours.

——————— **CLIENT STORY** ———————

I've always had a love and appreciation for horses and felt they were very intuitive animals. When the opportunity came up to work with Myra and Gestalt, I knew I wanted to experience it for myself. What an amazing, beautiful experience. It's difficult to express the value that a horse or horses can bring to someone's life, but, for me, having the opportunity to work with the horses was a very personal, spiritual, emotional, touching, heartfelt, and healing journey. Ginger, Royal, and Annie were the special horses that I spent time with during my visit. Each horse was unique in his/her own way and highly intuitive, but they all met me where I was at in my journey. It was such an intimate experience that provided my mind, body, and soul a refreshed and renewed perspective, guidance on ways of managing grief—from significant loss of multiple miscarriages—all while keeping the faith and being able to move forward with an internal feeling of calmness and inner peace. I feel incredibly blessed to have had this life-changing experience with the horses and forever grateful for the personal growth and awareness that has come along with it. Thank you, Myra, Ginger, Royal, and Annie for all that you do in helping others heal while crossing life's bridges.

~ September

QUESTIONS FOR REFLECTION

1) What would you want to do to truly recharge and reignite your soul?
2) How can you shift your rhythm to make self-care a priority?
3) What can you do to pay it forward?

Conclusion

There is something about the outside of a horse
that is good for the inside of a man.

~ Winston Churchill

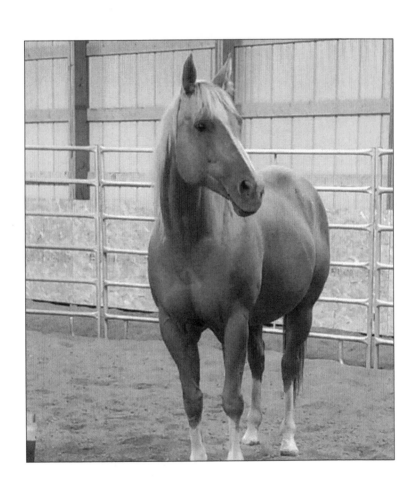

Whatever bridge you cross, whatever season of life you are in ...

- *Stay curious.* Keep your heart and mind open to possibilities. If you're open, life provides learning opportunities for growth every day.
- *Be connected.* Be a lifelong learner of YOU. Give yourself grace and self-compassion as you navigate your journey.
- *Seek clarity.* Declutter areas of your life and open your eyes to see opportunities. You'll improve your focus and sense of direction, sparking motivation for movement.
- *Shift with intention—bit by bit.* Move with purpose. Sometimes it's the little things in life that make the biggest difference.
- *Recharge and reignite.* Take care of yourself—unplug and unwind. Identify, embrace, and utilize your God-given gifts to serve others, creating a ripple effect of kindness and compassion.

This is one of my favorite poems. May your light continue to shine for all to see.

Our Deepest Fear—by Marianne Williamson

Our deepest fear is not that we are inadequate,
Our deepest fear is that we are powerful beyond measure.
It is our light, not our darkness
That most frightens us.

We ask ourselves
Who am I to be brilliant, gorgeous, talented, fabulous?
Actually, who are you not to be?
You are a child of God.

Your playing small
Does not serve the world.
There's nothing enlightened about shrinking
So that other people won't feel insecure around you.

We are all meant to shine,
As children do.
We were born to make manifest
The glory of God that is within us.

It's not just in some of us;
It's in everyone.

And as we let our own light shine,
We unconsciously give other people permission to do the same.
As we're liberated from our own fear,
Our presence automatically liberates others.

About the Author

Dr. Myra Heckenlaible-Gotto, EdD

*She dances to the songs in her head, speaks
with the rhythm of her heart,
and loves from the depths of her soul.*

~ Dean Jackson

Myra's extensive background as a teacher and psychologist has prepared her for many of life's challenges, but her faith has been her stronghold. She has used her mind, heart, and spirit to fulfill her higher purpose of helping others find their higher good. In her professional career of more than thirty-five years, Myra has worked with people in all stages of life's journey—children, adolescents, and adults—in a variety of educational and mental health settings. She has been a special education teacher, school psychologist, visiting assistant professor, licensed psychologist, and registered play therapist.

As she grew in her understanding of human development, she began to seek alternative ways to help those seeking personal growth, self-awareness, and healing. To follow her calling, her focus shifted to her coaching practice, blending her heart for teaching, love for horses and nature, and passion for helping others. She combined her knowledge in human growth with her love of horses by becoming a Certified Practitioner of the Equine Gestalt Coaching Method ®. To further expand her services in self-awareness and leadership, she also became a GiANT Certified Guide (Leadership Coach) through GiANT Worldwide. In God's timing, her training and career experiences led her to where she is today. Myra now incorporates a variety of approaches into her work.

Throughout her life and career, Myra has always been a very curious individual—eager to learn, willing to step outside the box, and committed to following her heart. Her underlying passion for helping people become aware of, embrace, and utilize their God-given gifts while letting go of things that hold them back, led to the creation of Crossing Life's Bridges.

Throughout her life's journey, one thing has remained true. At the core of her foundation lies the little farm girl from South Dakota—and her faith.

CONTACT CROSSING LIFE'S BRIDGES

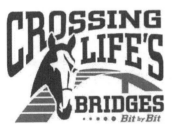

Website:
CrossingLifesBridges.com
Email:
myra@crossinglifesbridges.com
Phone:
507-822-3177

For up-to-date information and upcoming events, follow us at

Facebook: facebook.com/CrossingLifesBridges
LinkedIn: linkedin.com/in/CrossingLifesBridges

About
Crossing Life's Bridges

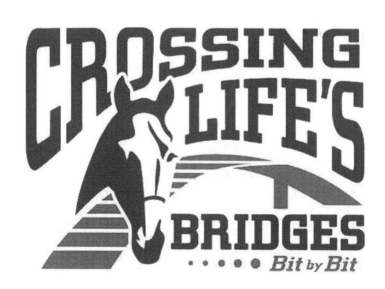

Crossing Life's Bridges was created for those who seek self-awareness, personal growth, guidance through life transitions, healing, recharge and renewal, and leadership development.

A variety of services are available to meet you where you are and may include a combination of experiential and learning modalities. You'll be given the opportunity to deepen your self-awareness and let go of things that hold you back as you stretch and grow, personally and professionally. Services are tailored to your needs and can be offered in a variety of settings and formats. In-person options include private sessions, workshops, and retreats. Sessions including horses take place in the arena at Crossing Life's Bridges. Additional services include online individual and group coaching and speaking engagements.

CONTACT CROSSING LIFE'S BRIDGES

Website:
CrossingLifesBridges.com
Email:
myra@crossinglifesbridges.com
Phone:
507-822-3177

For up-to-date information and upcoming events, follow us at

Facebook: facebook.com/CrossingLifesBridges
LinkedIn: linkedin.com/in/CrossingLifesBridges

I felt it would be beneficial to share a brief explanation of my current certifications:

Certified Practitioner in the Equine Gestalt Coaching Method®

The Equine Gestalt Coaching Method ® is experiential in nature and involves the horse as an active partner with the coach in the client's exploratory process. No previous horse experience is necessary to participate or benefit from the experience.

If you're seeking personal growth, feel out of sorts given a life transition, or need to recharge and reignite yourself, I invite you to call me for a free exploratory call to discuss your needs and possible options. The horses and I look forward to meeting you at Crossing Life's Bridges for an Equine Gestalt Coaching session or event.

If you want to experience an Equine Gestalt Coaching session but aren't able to come to Crossing Life's Bridges, I encourage you to contact http://www.TouchbyaHorse.com to find a Certified Equine Gestalt Coach near you.

GiANT Certified Guide (Leadership Coach)
GiANT Worldwide is a global media and content development company specializing in leadership transformation. If you're seeking personal or professional development for your small business or yourself, I welcome the opportunity to visit with you to discuss your needs and share possibilities.

To get a glimpse of what GiANT has to offer, I invite you to create a free GiANT account by using my GiANT affiliate code, https://www.giant.tv/myraheckenlaible-gotto. You'll have access to a wealth of information and valuable resources to help you deepen your self-awareness, improve your communication skills, and strengthen your ability to relate to others. I'll then connect with you to see how I can further serve you.

For large corporations who're ready to grow their leaders, teams, and organizations, I encourage you to go to www.giantworldwide.com to find a certified guide/consultant who specializes in large corporations.